New Evangelization

LEONARDO BOFF

New Evangelization
Good News to the Poor

Translated from the Portuguese by
Robert R. Barr

ORBIS BOOKS

Maryknoll, New York 10545

The Catholic Foreign Mission Society of America (Maryknoll) recruits and trains people for overseas missionary service. Through Orbis Books, Maryknoll aims to foster the international dialogue that is essential to mission. The books published, however, reflect the opinions of their authors and are not meant to represent the official position of the society.

First published as *Nova Evangelização: Perspectiva dos Oprimidos*
© 1990 by Editora Vozes, Av. Tristão Gonçalves, 1158, 60015 Fortaleza, CE, Brazil

This edition published in the United States by Orbis Books, Maryknoll, NY 10545, and in Great Britain by Burns & Oates, Wellwood, North Farm Rd., Tunbridge Wells, Kent TN2 3DR

Library of Congress Cataloging-in-Publication Data

Boff, Leonardo.
    [Nova evangelização. English]
    New evangelization : good news to the poor /
  Leonardo Boff ; translated from the Portuguese by Robert R. Barr.
    p. cm.
    Translation of: Nova evangelização.
    ISBN 0-88344-778-9
    1. Evangelistic work—Latin America. 2. Liberation theology.
  3. Catholic Church—Missions—Latin America—History. 4. Indians,
  Treatment of—Latin America—History. 5. Church work with the poor—
  Catholic Church. 6. Latin America—Church history. I. Title.
  BV3777.L3B6413   1991
  266'.28—dc20
                                        91-30804
                                            CIP

"Alas! Let us sorrow at their coming!

"They have christianized us. But they have passed us from one owner to another like animals.

"Only in a mad time, by insane priests, was sorrow instituted among us, was 'Christianity' instituted among us. The many Christians came here, with their true God: but this was the beginning of our misery, the beginning of tribute, the beginning of begging, the cause of hidden discord, the beginning of battles with firearms, the beginning of our trampling, the beginning of our total stripping, the beginning of debtor slavery, the beginning of flogging for indebtedness, the beginning of everlasting quarrels, the beginning of suffering. It was the beginning of the work of the Spaniards and the priests, the beginning of the use of the chiefs, the schoolmasters, and the overseers.

"They have taught us fear, they have come to make the flowers wither. That their flower might live, they have broken off our blossom and swallowed it down."

The gospel seen as antigospel by the Maya, recorded in the book of Chilam Balam.

The best service to our fellows is evangelization, which disposes them to fulfill themselves as children of God, liberates them from injustices, and fosters their integral advancement.

Puebla Final Document, no. 1145

Contents

PART 2
MINIMUM CONTENT FOR A NEW
EVANGELIZATION   61

PART 3
THE LIBERATIVE METHOD OF OUR LADY
OF GUADALUPE: THE AMERINDIAN GOSPEL   93

Preface:
A New Evangelization –
A Debt Owed
to Latin America

Many debts are owing in Latin America today.[1]

Economic debt has risen to a figure in the billions of dollars, indemnifying the large financial conglomerates at extremely heavy cost to the people in terms of social poverty. This debt must be reviewed, and either not paid in its totality or refinanced at lower interest rates.

Political debt takes social and political forms of institutionalized violence marginalizing the *campesinos*, privileging capital, and burdening labor. This entails the violation of human rights, especially those of the poor, the young, blacks, and Indians. This debt will be paid to Latin America only when the sovereignty of capital is abolished and an authentic democracy introduced here, with majority rule and popular participation.

Cultural debt. The culture of the Iberian invaders either destroyed the "witness-cultures" of the natives or reduced them to isolated pockets of resistance, traumatizing Latin Americans down to our own day. Only through respect and support for the cultures of the natives, blacks, mestizos, and the poor generally, shall we ever be able to repay a part of this debt.

Anthropological debt. Colonization meant not only the domination of bodies, but the defeat of souls as well, through the nonrecognition of the other as other. That other was violently europeanized, and education and catechesis meant a process of accommodation to the culture of the dominator. This debt can only be paid through a recognition of the existence of the other, the value of that other, and the equal dignity of the culture of that other.

Ethico-religious debt. As an aggregate of poor countries, Latin America is shunted to the sidelines of the overall development process—abandoned to its own technologies and authoritarian social forms, its silent cultures and unacknowledged religions, its strict military control, its National Security doctrines for the preservation of institutional disorder. This ethico-religious debt will only be paid when the Latin American peoples become the agents of their own destiny, creating social relations and values that express their own cultural roots.

Finally, there is a debt of *evangelization*. The evangelization that occurred here entailed the transposition of the institutions, symbols, concepts, and moral habits of European Christian culture to a new continent. By and large, there was no encounter between faith and native reality, between gospel and autochthonous cultures, which would have permitted the rise of a Christian expression typically ours. Only popular Catholicism, the fruit of the people's creativity, subsisting on the margins of official Catholicism, has meant an original creation of the faith, an island in a sea of domination that extends to every corner of society. This debt will only be paid when conditions are right for attempting a liberative evangelization, an evangelization from a point of departure in the cultural matrices of a poor, deeply religious people. This seems to be the sense of the "new evangelization" now under way.

The expression was coined by John Paul II, on March 9, 1983, in Port-au-Prince, Haiti, on the occasion of the Nineteenth General Assembly of the Latin American Bishops' Conference. The pope said:

> The commemoration of a half-millennium of evangelization will have its full meaning if there is a commitment . . . not of reevangelization, but of a new evangelization—new in its fervor, in its methods, and in its expression.[2]

As may be seen from this statement, it is not a matter of prolonging the evangelization that has always prevailed in Latin America, with certain reforms, and accompanied by the processes of renewal with which we are familiar in the traditional schema, omitting any structural changes. It is a matter of a new project. It does not entail a critical judgment to be handed down on the evangelization that took place beginning in the sixteenth century. But the implication is that the new evangelization will seek to maintain its distance from its predecessor, as if to say that the latter was and is insufficient—inadequate to the challenges perceived nowadays on our continent. Therefore it is styled a *new evangelization*.

According to the pope, the new evangelization must be accompanied by a new *fervor*. Fervor is not a kind of spontaneous combustion. Fervor is aroused by the identification of a great cause. Fervor is the enthusiasm and the courage to confront all manner of difficulty with cheerfulness. As can be gathered from the documents of Medellín (1968) and Puebla (1979), foundational texts for the pastoral work of the Latin American local and regional churches, an ecclesial awareness has identified the great cause of our continent: how to produce the good news of Jesus amid a social reality in ruins. The "good news" will be good only if transformations occur in these miserable social realities: if instead of unfair they become humane, instead of being unjust they become social relations productive of justice and participation. How do local and regional churches assist in these transformations, that they may be genuinely productive of good news, and hence the proclamation of a plenitude that only the gospel can offer? A brief, precise definition of its task has been and still is: liberation for communion and participation in society and the church. In the conditions in which the Latin American peoples suffer, such a cause will triumph only if there is fervor. It is this fervor that is transforming the entire church community into a collective agent of evangelization. It fosters the emergence of poor who are aware and liberative, and occasions the appearance of prophets filled with a holy wrath at the iniquity of the political and social order implanted here, and full of deeds of consolation for the oppressed. This is the fervor that has inspired so many with the courage to sacrifice their lives for their humiliated, offended sisters and brothers. Our Latin American churches today, almost all of them, are martyr churches.

The new evangelization must be new in its *methods*, the pope assures us. Not only the content must be new; the method must be new as well. In other words, the way in which we produce the good news belongs to the very nature of the good news. Contact with the person and message of Jesus ought to generate an atmosphere of benevolence, of a geometrical growth of all that is human, worthy, and desirable for body and soul. This can be achieved only if the message is participatory: only if the dichotomy between evangelizer and evangelized is overcome, in an evangelization that involves everyone; only if we renounce all cultural imposition in the name of the gospel; only if we foster the assimilation of the good news of Jesus from a point of departure in the matrices of the various cultures present on our continent, beginning with the culture of the dominated, since it is they, evangelically, who must always be the first addressees and prime agents of evangelization.

Finally, the new evangelization will have to be new in its *expressions*. The expressions of evangelization must be products of the cultures themselves, and not simply—as they have been over the past five hundred years—reproductions of European cultures to be adopted by Tupi-Guarani, Aymara, or Aztec natives who understand nothing of Latin or of a liturgical ceremonial springing from the cultural experience of Byzantium, Rome, and Aix-la-Chapelle. Evangelization must begin to respect the inalienable right of all persons to know, praise, and serve the God of history with the instruments of their own culture and the symbols of their own traditions. This right does not enjoy full freedom of exercise. This is why we have only an official Catholicism, of Roman coinage, and not multiple "Catholicisms" legitimately expressing the gospel through a multiplicity of cultures. The new evangelization must produce the fruit of a Latin American, ecumenical Christianity, a Christianity whose visage portrays the cultural profiles of all who coexist on this continent.

The new evangelization must generate life for the great masses who languish in foul, scandalously inadequate living conditions. The first thing that evangelization will mean in Latin America is saving the lives of the poor. Without this liberative dimension, there will be no good news worthy of the name, no good news re-presenting the memory of the practice of Jesus and the apostles.

Today we must never forget the criticism lodged against Christians of the sixteenth century by natives who accused them of proclaiming a "cruel, unjust, and ruthless god." Evangelization under the sign of colonialism failed to prevent the genocide that attended the wars, the abuse, the slave labor, the European diseases to which the natives had no resistance. Between 1500 and 1600, the native population was reduced by a ratio of 20 to 1: in 1519, when Hernán Cortés reached the plateau of Anahuac in Mexico, some 25,200,000 persons were living there; by 1595 only 1,375,000 remained.[3]

Against the background of this genocide, the new evangelization must make the connection God-poor-liberation altogether clear, in opposition to the connection that predominated for centuries: God-powerful-domination.

A modern analyst writes of what the Iberian invasion meant for Latin America:

> It is here, if anywhere, that the word "genocide" is applicable. Here, it seems to me, we have a "world record," and not only in relative terms (the destruction was on the order of ninety percent and more), but in absolute terms, as well, inasmuch as we are speaking of a plunge in population estimated at 70 million (in a Latin America numbering 80 million, and a world population of about 400 million). No twentieth-century massacre is comparable with this hecatomb. No wonder the efforts of certain authors to dissipate the so-called black legend, which lays the responsibility of this genocide at the door of Spain and thus besmirches that country's fine reputation, will be in vain. It is the fact that is "black," not the legend.[4]

Once an accomplice of the death machine, today Christianity must become the ally of the promotion of life in the victims of a type of "development" that excludes the masses. Today's suffering is the consequence of the happenings of five hundred years ago. The colonial invasion is still in full swing, in the form of technological domination, in the form of the capital that enters our continent to exploit cheap labor and an abundance of raw materials, and in the form of policies that favor the mighty of the world and their allies at home and tread the people under foot.[5]

The new evangelization, whose first beginnings date from the 1960s, and which addresses first of all the dominated peoples, has not yet struck sufficiently deep root. It has not yet managed to convince the victims it prioritizes. What certain Andean Indians did to Pope John Paul II, when he was visiting Peru in 1985, is symptomatic. Maximo Flores, of the Kollosuyo (Aymara) Indian movement, Emmo Valeriano, of the (Aymara) Indian Party, and Ramiro Reynaga, of the (Kheswa) Tupac Katari Indian movement, delivered a letter to the pontiff. It read, in part:

We, the Indians of the Andes and America, have decided to take the opportunity of this visit by John Paul II to return him his Bible. In five centuries, it has brought us neither love, nor peace, nor justice. Please take your Bible back, and return it to our oppressors. It is they, rather than we, who have need of its moral precepts. Since the arrival of Christopher Columbus, a culture, a language, a religion of Europe, and the very values of Europe have been imposed on America by force.[6]

In his public explanation of the letter, Reynaga maintained:

The Bible came to us as part of the colonial project of constraint. It was the ideological weapon of that colonial assault. The Spanish sword, which attacked and murdered the bodies of the Indian by day, was transformed by night into a cross to attack the Indians' souls.

How can these accusations, these just complaints on the part of the Indians, grave as they are, be refuted? These are the victims filing this indictment, not some rancorous intellectual or frustrated cleric, and they deserve to be heard and respected. The oppressed are appealing for our evangelization—begging us for reasons to go on living, reasons to fight for life. Unfortunately, our debt of justice to the natives, the blacks, and the outcast remains unpaid even today. Our churches must pay it. And that is the reason for this book.

PART 1 | Evangelizing from Oppressed Cultures

In some circles, a discussion of the "evangelization of cultures"—which ought rather to be "evangelization and cultures"—serves as a ploy to escape the reality that has dominated discussion in pastoral theology in recent years: the reality of the poor, oppressed, and outcast. This debate has culminated in the preferential option for the poor, an option against their poverty, and today constitutes, without a doubt, the trademark of the local and regional churches of Latin America.

The reality of the poor is charged with conflict. The poor are made poor by economic mechanisms, social relations, and discriminations that all offend against justice. An understanding of society, the churches, and theology on the basis of this reality becomes a further point of conflict, in that it enables us to perceive both the complicity of all three of these bodies in the oppression of the poor and their solidarity with their battles for life and liberty.

The abiding poverty of the poor, indeed the present aggravation of their misery, betrays a certain failure on the part of traditional evangelization. Not without reason, then, do we hear of a new evangelization, an evangelization that will be more involved with the lot of the poor, an evangelization capable not only of proclaiming the good news of liberation but of assisting in its production as well. Finally, it is important to understand that the oppression of persons today is the ultimate fruit of that process of conquest, subjugation, and domination that started in the sixteenth century and has not yet ended. If in 1992, in the process of recalling the fifth centenary of this event, we fail to maintain a vivid awareness of this contradiction, we shall only be rubbing salt into the wounds of all those persons who, in the rough but realistic words of historian Capistrano de Abreu, are the "buried and buried again, bled and bled again" of our history.

What I wish to do in this book is to begin with the brutal, une-quivocal fact: the poor are suffering more than ever. In nearly all Latin American countries, the poor are dying off even more rapidly than they were when the bishops met at Medellín (1968) and Puebla (1979). This calls us to account. It must not be ignored, or spiritualized, or dissolved into some other reality, and thereby seem to lose its character as a scandal that cries out for amends. If we begin with the reality of cultures,[1] then we must keep the following in mind from the outset: it is in the interest of the liberation of these oppressed that we make use of every possible theoretical consideration. We must not shrink from such considerations, or distract ourselves with other approaches, which may be interesting but will have the ultimate result that the churches will falter in their commitment to justice and real liberation. Let us not speak of roses when doing so will render us oblivious of the suffering of the gardener.

Let me pass directly to the subject of an evangelization that begins with the oppressed, marginalized cultures.[2]

1 | Cultures, Acculturation, Enculturation, Inculturation, and Civilization: Semantic Precision

There are more than three hundred current definitions of culture.[3] There is the famous definition by the North American anthropologist Edward Tylor in 1871, which reads:

> Taken in its broad ethnographic sense, culture is the entire complex of cognitions, beliefs, arts, morality, laws, customs, or any other capacity or habits acquired by man as a member of a society.

This concept is correct in what it says, but reductionistic in what it does not say. Culture embraces more than the world of symbols and significations. That world is rooted in the material world, in the social world, and in the human imagination, of individuals and collectivities alike. Accordingly, culture must be understood in a far more integral sense.[4] Meanwhile, Tylor's concept has become the current one. When we read, for example, that the pope has met with "the world of culture," what is meant is that he has met with intellectuals and artists — persons who manage ideas, create symbols, and produce cognitions. This is a restricted meaning of "culture."

Anthropologists have fashioned a far wider-ranging understanding of culture, with the object of doing justice to the many-sided phenomenon of human cultures. There is no such thing as culture in the singular. Concretely, there are only cultures, in the plural. "Culture," in the singular, is a highly abstract concept. Its raison d'être is merely to stand in contradistinction from other, equally theoretical, concepts, like "nature," for example. Thus, we hear of a "zero-degree culture."

In this sense, by way of a generalization, by "zero-degree culture" we understand everything we do either as individuals (men or women) or as a collectivity; as well as what is done *with* us, and everything that, actively and passively, we seek to signify to ourselves and communicate to others.

Human life is always cultural — just by being human. It is immersed in the nature that is manifested within and without human life. It "works" that nature, and transforms it into, precisely, culture. For example, agriculture is the work a human being does in the "field." A person "works on" amorphous nature, separating a part of it, developing it, and transforming it by means of work in the fields — hence the word "agriculture," meaning "culture of the field" (from the Latin *ager* and *cultura*). Human life has an infinitude of dimensions. And in all of these dimensions there is culture, because in all of them there is human toil, which always begins with something that is not cultural but natural, or at least something that reworks and "transignifies" what has already been rendered cultural:

— *on the cosmic level*, inasmuch as human beings (individually and collectively) find themselves inserted into the process of creation, and so create their habitat;

— *on the personal level*, corresponding to the irreducibility of singular human existence, especially in the exercise of their freedom;

— *on the economic level*, that of the production and reproduction of material life;

— *on the political level*, that of the various forms of human coexistence;

— *on the symbolical level*, which concerns the significations and values we attribute to human practices, and to everything that enters into a relationship with the human world;

— *on the religious level*, through which is projected an ultimate meaning, transcending all singular meanings and embracing the whole of reality.

Each human group develops all of these instances in its own way. All human beings work, all cook, all eat, all organize themselves socially, all create symbols, codes, and significations, but each collectivity does so in its own way and manner. Hence cultural plurality. Why this cultural plurality? Could not human beings be programed like beavers or bees, which have been building their habitat in the same way for thousands of centuries? The fact is that the activity of these collective artificers is genetically determined. This is why they always build their products in the same way. They have no *praxis*. Praxis is the product of human reflection and will. Human beings, unlike animals, even the higher ones, are characterized by praxis, which presupposes the ability to reflect, to project, to signify, and to transform. Through this praxis, nature is transformed into culture. That is to say, the logic of determination is replaced by that of spontaneity, and of a complex of significations and values. Culture is more than a mere process of adaptation of nature to human desires. It is also a language, which communicates significations and values. A car is more than just a means of transportation. It also communicates a social meaning: it reveals a person's status, aesthetic preferences, and so on.

Human beings work not only upon nature, but upon themselves as well. This makes them more than gregarious animals (like wolves or primates): they are "social" beings. They emerge from the order of biological necessities governed by determination (ants have their rigid division of labor, chimpanzees their internal hierarchies and stereotyped patterns of mutual assistance, agreement, and rejection), to enter the order of liberty, of free choice, of selection among various possible alternatives, and of the subjective assimilation of the imperative of their natural impulses, as they impose order and rule on these. In this social field, freely and consensually, classifications, behavior codes, orderings, and principles of relationship are established. Human beings are no longer mere beings of nature. Through culture, they become *subjects*, who have rights and duties, who originate practices that transform or conserve nature and society, and who originate symbols, significations, and values.

From what has been said, it should be clear that culture pervades us entirely, in all our dimensions. We cannot, therefore, restrict culture to the so-called cultural world (that of schools, arts, folklore, religion—the world of ideas and values). Everything is steeped in culture—even physical work, economics, politics, and the production of symbols. Thus, we rightly speak of *material culture* (the series of instruments and technology whereby we ensure our survival), *social culture* (power relationships, rules of behavior, the social division of work), *symbolical culture* (the significations given to things, philosophies and doctrines, popular and national festivals).

Everything human constitutes a source of culture. However, in ranking these forces, we emphasize four of them that are especially powerful and distinctive: work, power, imagination, and religion. It will be superfluous to observe that these four forces are always interrelated. An authentic inclusive dialectic prevails among them (a *perichoresis,* to borrow a theological term): where one is, there are the others as well.

Work, whether subjective or objective (see John Paul II, *Laborem Exercens*, no. 6) is one of the most fundamental constructive factors of culture. In the words of Vatican II, work "flows immediately from the person, assigning a framework to the things of nature" (*Gaudium et Spes*, no. 67). Work is always social, being performed within a particular social division, and is interpreted in the most diverse significations (for moderns it is a means of domestication of nature; for natives a form of assisting Mother Earth, Pachamama). The way in which work is organized, whether in a regime of collaboration or exploitation, enjoying a primacy over capital or subordinated to it, will characterize social coexistence in a given time and space.

Power is another force that promotes culture. At the political level, there are authoritarian, charismatic, or democratic social relations of power. Relations of power can be those of appropriation, expropriation, control, consolidation or debilitation of interests, or the imposition of principles regulating conduct by some groups over others. It is in access to power or exclusion from it that dominant and dominated cultures arise, cultures of silence, and popular cultures. To ignore conflicts of power, particularly in a history as marked by inequality as that of Latin America, would mean concealing a fundamental datum, a decisive one for any process of liberation and liberative evangelization.

Another powerful force in the building of culture is *imagination*. Through their imagination, human beings constantly add something new to the sheer, sometimes brutal, fact of reality.

Thereby they create interpretations, discover new connections, and construct life meanings. Imagination is the font of creativity, including scientific creativity. Social imagination is especially important. Here is the source of a collectivity's dreams, utopias, and projects of coexistence. It is imagination that confers color on human experiences. Imagination is the faculty of seeing, feeling, and desiring something beyond what is given in these experiences. Imagination never tires, manifesting itself in festival, play, and rite.

Finally, we have *religion*. Through religion, societies define for themselves the most transcendent meanings of their practices, and the destiny of persons and history. The vehicles of religions are powerful symbols, archetypes of great depth as well as of historical permanence. It is by way of religion that separations are repaired and points of convergence discovered between times and eras. It is in religion, rather than in philosophy, that the human quest for ultimate meaning and a final consummation of creation and the human heart find their themes, symbols, rites, and celebration. Thus, all culture develops its religions, as well,[5] intertwining them with the other forces, such as power (in the religious expressions of the dominant groups, the subordinate groups, and so forth), or various particular regimes of work, with the result that, even in religion, a social division of work arises (division between clergy and laity); and so on.

Complex as the subject of cultures may be, we must not forget our basic question. To what extent does culture promote liberation, consolidate oppression, hinder a defiant conscientization, and foster or impede life and freedom?

The expression "dominant cultures and dominated cultures" does not convey the entire, complex problematic of the human cultural phenomenon. But in the Latin American context (and in that of the vast majority of humanity) this aspect of culture is of supreme importance, as it inhibits or cancels all other cultural expressions. "Dominant" and "dominated" are not just extrinsic categories, but intrinsic ones as well. Domination is possible only when the dominator succeeds in penetrating the dominated, and thereby making them accept their situation. The dominated *host* the dominator within themselves, as part of their reality. We can understand, then, how division permeates persons, institutions, the imagination, and religion. Domination prevents dominated groups from producing an autonomous culture that expresses their identity. Under what conditions is work performed? What kind of religion will the dominated be able to develop? Imagination alone is their great field of freedom. Not without reason have the great libertarian utopias and the most radical dreams of transformation been projected by dominated groups.

This situation is that of the great majorities of our continent and the whole of humanity. What does it mean, in this framework, to evangelize cultures? Either the gospel furthers the promotion of a cultural dynamism among the oppressed and marginalized, a free dynamism, one that fosters life and freedom; or else, for lack of analysis, out of naivety, or under pressure from special interests, it becomes an accomplice of the maintenance of an unjust status quo. I wish to maintain this perspective through all these reflections. It is a humanistic, ethical, religious, and evangelical perspective. On the basis of this option, we shall attempt to gain an understanding of the extremely complex problem of cultures, without letting the anthropological complexity of the cultural phenomenon, of such concern to anthropologists, distract from our basic liberative concern.

With this as background, let me now identify certain frequently recurrent, more or less clear, and related concepts:

Enculturation, also called internalization or socialization, is the process by which the members of a given culture assimilate their values, their codes, their habits, and their understanding of the world.

The *inculturation* of the gospel is the process by which a culture assimilates the gospel in terms of its own cultural matrices. Only with inculturation is there authentic evangelization — an encounter between a particular culture and the evangelical aspirations.

Acculturation is the process undergone by a culture when it enters into contact with another culture, adapts to it, and assimilates its elements in terms of its own matrices.

Transculturation is a forced acculturation (by way of physical or symbolical violence), such as the Amerindian natives suffered under the impact of the conquest and expansion of the Christian system that prevailed in Spain and Portugal.

Transcultural is used in this book in a positive sense, to denote the character of certain human values that permeate the various cultures and account for the specificity of the human being qua human, like the capacity to defend justice, to implement solidarity, to offer love, and so on.

Civilization denotes a series of values and practices calculated to promote the common good of the human species and concretized in various cultures, such as justice, the defense of life, solidarity with the weak, respect for the other, and so on. Since Paul VI, we have often heard of a "civilization of love," and since John Paul II of a "civilization of solidarity," as an antidote to selfishness at the international level, and as an incentive to the preservation of creation and the peaceful coexistence among peoples. Today, all cultures ought to be civilized. That is, they should be cultures that renounce domination over others, and respect and accept the values of others. The gospel is an important factor in civilization, as it fosters the practice of love, fellowship, and a belief in the divine filiation of all human creatures.

Having provided these necessary explanations, I must now broach the questions: Is there such a thing as a Latin American culture? What is the relationship between gospel and cultures in Latin America?

2 | Latin American Culture and Its Catholic Substrate: Myth and Reality

Amerindia (Abia Yala, or "ripe land," the name the Kuna Indians of Panama give to America) had been populated for at least forty thousand years when the Iberians invaded and occupied it. Great cultures had arisen here, based on maize. There were empires here, centers of power with hierarchical governments and millions of citizens. But let us omit pre-Columbian Amerindia. Let us restrict ourselves to the current situation. Is there such a thing today as a Latin American culture[6] unifying the continent and calling for a unified strategy of evangelization?

We must recognize that, from the cultural viewpoint, Latin America is an extremely complex, indeed contradictory, reality. In the terminology of anthropologist Darcy Ribeiro, living here in tension and conflict are the "witness peoples," the "new peoples," the "transplanted peoples," and the "emerging peoples." All of these peoples have a common denominator: the colonial invasion of the sixteenth century and its consequences down to the present day. The great Amerindian cultures were partly exterminated and partly subjected to the point of almost completely losing, through the trauma of violence, the memory of their past grandeur.

According to some critical historians, Latin America has been the victim of three successive invasions, all with the same cultural effect: oppression, distortion, and a harnessing to other cultures. With a touch of exaggeration (but with a core of truth), we might say that the Latin America of today is an invention of European cultural and capitalist expansionism. For the Iberians, America was an obstacle along their way to the Orient, as they sailed in quest of new commercial fields and greater military power with a view to attacking the Muslims along the coasts.

10

Accordingly, as peoples, as cultural, economic, political, and ideological organizations, Latin America constitutes a reflex of the capitalistic European culture that today, along with North America and Japan, has the hegemony over Western politics and policy. We have always been dependent on external centers of domination. As a result we still have difficulty defining our identity, which is either rendered impossible, or found to be alienated or deeply divided. We have a culture of fragments, of the flotsam of something that once was whole. There is no escaping the fact: we are a broken mirror, a tragic, unhappy consciousness obliged to see itself in the mirror of others, violently maintained in a state of underdevelopment and thereby deprived of the necessary means to be sovereigns of our own history.[7]

Even the celebrated "radically Catholic substrate" of "Latin American culture" is a consequence of the conquest of souls. It represents the Iberian Catholic model, and not the fruit of an encounter of the gospel with our cultures in an atmosphere of dialogue, equality, and cross-fertilization. What has predominated has been the conquest of bodies by the colonial invasion, the conquest of souls by the mission, and the conquest of consciences by the imposition of the morality of Iberian Catholicism.[8]

The first invasion occurred in the sixteenth century, with Spanish and Portuguese colonization. This meant the subjugation of the Indians, with the consequent paralysis of an autonomous civilizing process. Then came the enslavement of the blacks, transported from Africa like animals. The purpose of the colonial enterprise was to enrich the metropolis, and secondarily to generate in Latin America a reproduction of the metropolitan culture (as we see from our geographical names: a New Spain, a New Granada, a New Santiago, and so on).

The second invasion took place in the nineteenth century. The political independence of the Latin American nations from the Iberian powers was accompanied by a profound economic integration into the capitalist system, then under the hegemony of England and France. Enormous contingents of Europeans arrived in America, as the European populations had exceeded the capacity of the industrial capitalist system to absorb them and make them produce. From the viewpoint of the black and the Indian, this invasion was violent as well, since they were left in the lurch where progress was concerned and condemned by the ideology of *embranquecimento*, or "whitening" of culture. Succeeding generations created islands of prosperity for themselves, typically by exploiting the cheap labor of the blacks or expropriating the lands of the Amerindians.

The third invasion began in the 1930s—to be consolidated from the 1960s—when military dictatorships were installed in the principal countries of the continent. The national bourgeoisies now struck an alliance with the large American, European, and Japanese conglomerates. Capitalistic relations penetrated everywhere, even in rural areas, creating social inequalities and levels of impoverishment unequaled in our history. First the Latin American countries had been subordinated to the colonial export of raw materials. Then they had been caught up in an industrial production and process of modernization whose benefits all went abroad. Now they were forced under the yoke of the financial centers of the capitalist metropolises, and saw themselves obliged to export any strong currencies they might have acquired (dollars, deutschmarks, and yen). This gave rise to an ever more cruel and inhuman dependency on the multinational corporations.

In order to support dizzying rates of capital accumulation, the National Security regimes were inaugurated. As we know, the "security" in question has always been that of capital, for whose sake these regimes commandeered the states and their apparatus. The states' favorite language to their citizens has been violence. Even after the slow, gradual overtures to a bourgeois liberal democracy, the armed forces have remained in control. The "democracies" are really *democraduras*—liberal democracies at the service of a dictatorship of the dominant class propped up by the military. This sociopolitical framework has opened the way for a culture of mass consumption, a mentality fostered by the modern communications media. The traditional cultures see themselves deprived of legitimacy, while offshoots of a popular culture arise linked to the organized struggle of workers and popular movements, within which are also found the base church communities and the sociopastoral ministries.

In the face of this complex, contradictory process, can one speak of *a* Latin American culture? If by culture we understand, as explained above, the various ways of organizing work, social life, the symbolical world, religion, and ecology, then we must say that the continental hegemony is still in the hands of a dependent and exclusive capitalist order, coexisting with the wreckage of other orders — of the Indian, of the slave system, of feudalism, of the forms of bare subsistence of popular strata condemned to misery.

Latin American culture as a meaningful identity is a myth. The colonial and neocolonial invasion, which is still going on today, has reached to the heart of the forces that produce culture. Everywhere is division, the infiltration of the invader into the world of the invaded, the fundamental duality of native and foreign. Despite this process of domination, we can say that, in many resistance and liberation movements among Indians and blacks, as well as workers and intellectuals integrated into these movements, the germs of a Latin American culture, a future convergence of Indians, blacks, mestizos, and immigrant peoples, is underway in seminal form.

What is the place of evangelization in this framework?

3 | Christianity in the Cultures of Latin America

I shall make no attempt to rehearse the extremely complex history of the evangelization, successful or failed, of the cultures of our continent. Generally speaking, it must be said that no encounter of cultures has occurred between that of the invader and those already present in the Amerindian lands. What there has been is actually a confrontation, and a destruction of otherness. The Christian religion has played its part in this drama. Catechesis has followed the line of the colonial project. The European ecclesiastical system was installed. Without exception, the missionaries identified the *orbis Christianus* with the order willed by God for the universe. The church was directly identified with the reign of God. The pope and the emperor were God's representatives to all human beings. We shall see this more clearly below.

Catechesis did not take place in a framework or spirit of intercultural dialogue. It meant the implantation of a model of Christianity that had already been constructed. There was no awareness of this model as a cultural product of Europe. It was understood as a revelation of God. Thus, it had nothing to learn from contact with the Indian or with any other culture. It had only to be given. The missionaries regarded missionary preaching and expansion as a matter of divine right. Opposition to the missionaries' activity was adequate cause for a "just war."[9]

All missionaries, even the most prophetic, like Pedro de Córdoba (author of *Christian Doctrine for the Instruction and Formation of the Indians, after the Manner of a History*, 1510) and Bartolomé de Las Casas (*The Sole Manner of Drawing All Peoples to the True Religion*, 1537) begin with the presupposition that Christianity is the only true religion: the Indians' religions are not only false, they are the work of Satan. Method alone is open to discussion: whether to use violence and force (the common method, which went hand in hand with colonialism), or a "delicate, soft, and sweet" method (in the words of Las Casas). Either method was calculated to achieve the same effect: conversion. There is no theological reading of the cultures and religions of the Indians. The only order willed by God is that of Christianity. All persons must be compelled to assimilate this religious order, which is also a cultural one.

Correlatively, as we study the first sixteenth-century catechisms (the pictorial ones, Pedro de Córdoba's, referred to above, the *Colloquies of the Twelve Apostles* of Bernardino de Sahagún, the catechetical writings of Alonso de Molina, Juan de la Anunciación, and others[10]), we perceive a constant: the satanization of the religions of the Indians. This repeated accusation produces infinite perplexity among the Aztecs and Incas. It is a genuine scandal. Always, on the part of both Spaniards and Portuguese, war is waged on the Indian shamans and priests. Mission is war on idolatry. The teachings of the Aztec ancestors, their legacy to those who were to come after them, "are all lies, vanity, fiction. They contain no truth."[11] Against the Mexican sages, the people's guides, the missionaries insist: "Know and hold for a surety that no one of all the gods you worship is God, the Giver of Life. All are devils of hell."[12] The missioners went so far as to understand the barbarity of the colonists as just punishment for sins of idolatry. And so they added a threat: "Unless you hear the divine words, . . . God, who has already begun to destroy you for your sins, will finally exterminate you altogether."[13]

Thus a strategy of fear prevailed. The first catechism developed on the continent, between 1510 and 1521, by Pedro de Córdoba's group in Santo Domingo, opened with the revelation of "a great secret, which you have never known or heard": that God has made heaven and hell. In heaven are all who have been converted to the Christian faith and have led a good life. And in hell are "all of your dead, all of your ancestors, your fathers, mothers, grandparents, relatives, and all who have existed and departed this life. And you shall go there as well, unless you become friends of God, and are baptized and become Christians, for all who are not Christians are God's enemies."[14] This is followed by gruesome descriptions of hell, and idyllic ones of heaven, with the object of persuading the Indians to embrace the Christian faith.

The Jesuits in Brazil testify: "Our experience is that it is very difficult to convert the Indians by love. But as this is a servile folk, fear accomplishes all."[15] Death and judgment were favored sermon topics, giving rise to the belief among the natives that the missionaries had the power to strike dead anyone they pleased. And so, as a Jesuit missionary testified, "some come to ask health, others to beg that we not cause them to die, out of a fear of us, as it has seemed to them that we indeed cause persons to die."[16] What gospel is this, based on the preaching of the reprobation of all in the past whom the natives held dear, on the satanization of what was most sacred to them—their religious traditions—on the terror of death, judgment, and hell?[17]

It is important that we make a theological critique of the kind of evangelization that was practiced at the moment of the founding of the church in Latin America. An analysis of the catechisms cited above reveals, on the strictly theological level, a profoundly questionable, and sometimes erroneous, theology. We see little of biblical inspiration, of Christianity as the history of God's visitation in grace and pardon. What prevails is the structure of Greek metaphysics—doctrinal, abstract, and universalistic. The missionaries work with a kind of metaphysics typical of the so-called ontotheology: on high, heaven, a place of delights, and here, at the center of the earth, hell, the place of pain and punishment (as in the first Latin American catechism, that of Pedro de Córdoba). The presentation of God follows rather the Greek philosophical scheme—that of the Supreme Being with his attributes—than the biblical one of a God in covenant with humanity (in Noah), with the people (in Abraham and Moses), with the heart of every person (according to the prophets), a God of tenderness for the poor (throughout the biblical tradition). Jesus is presented in metaphysical terms, his two natures, human and divine (seven articles of faith for each). There is nothing about a following of Jesus. The morality of the commandments is frankly casuistic, in the European ethical mold, and bereft of any concern for the ethics of Indian cultures (apart from a treatment of the sins peculiar to these cultures).

Theologically speaking, can we say that there was an evangelization here? It would be more correct to say that there was an expansion and implantation of European culture, which had assimilated the gospel in its own way and carried it in this already inculturated and limited form to the witness cultures of the natives. What there was, was a war of idolatries, and we could see this if we would take seriously the error prevailing in the minds of the missionaries and the native sages, respectively—namely, the identification of an image of God with the actual reality of God. Not a single missionary was aware of the fact that the God the church proclaimed was a cultural image, developed in a syncretism of biblical, Greco-Latin, and barbarian material, and not actually God, who always transcends language and representation. In the same fashion, the divinities of the Indian cultures were only representations of the mystery of God, of course, not actually God. The essence of idolatry is the identification of the reality of God with the image of God produced by a culture. And the missionaries blithely identified their image of God with God just as the natives did. Unless we undertake this kind of internal criticism, of a theological order, there is not the remotest hope that we shall ever achieve the formulation of a new evangelization.

The nineteenth century consolidated, and in some way radicalized, the kind of evangelization that had been implanted. By now Christianity had been centralized around the figure of the pope. The entire church had been romanized. To be a missionary meant to carry the Roman Catholic monolith everywhere you went. Converted peoples were not to be permitted to embark on a Christian culture project of their own: they had to adopt the determinations others had made concerning them, and often against them.

A crisis was in store for this model. It did not meet the ecclesial demands of the particular churches of Latin America. The Second Vatican Council inspired an ecclesiology focused on the value of the local churches and the inculturation of the gospel. This space of freedom permitted the emergence of Medellín and Puebla, which gave the first official encouragement to an evangelization in the patterns of popular culture, and from a starting point among the poor and dominated cultures. Only now is there a historical and ecclesial opportunity for the formation of a Latin American Catholicism with the characteristics of the various cultures present in Latin America, a Catholicism that will necessarily be distinct from the European, but open to it, and in communion with other Catholicisms that must arise in the various cultures as the fruit of an inculturation of the Christian message. Abandoning its old roles as accomplice of colonial and neocolonial domination, then prophetical scourge of the abuses of that enterprise (without questioning its legitimacy), then friend of isolated attempts to achieve autonomy through representatives of the church who supported and promoted the independence of our countries (like Morelos, Caneca, and others), Latin American Christianity is more and more frankly libertarian today. It encourages the full autonomy of the particular, while always in communion with and open to the universal.

Such was the course of the evangelization carried out officially by church authorities. Directly linked to the interests of dominating power, it had failed to produce an inculturation that would respect, enter into dialogue with, and assume the cultures present in Latin America. It consecrated a duplication of the Catholicism already inculturated in Europe.

There was, however, another kind of inculturation of the Christian faith, the one produced by popular Catholicism.[18] This is not a corruption of official Catholicism. But it does maintain its own profile, and rests heavily on devotion to the saints and on religious festivals. This kind of Catholicism has been developed not only by the clergy or the ecclesiastical establishment, but by the people, the laity, the devout. This new Catholicism has adopted popular culture: not being under the control of the official church, it can be inculturated into the universe of popular representations. Hence its greater authenticity: it represents an original creation of the Christian people of Latin America. It may be the only exception to the rule that the Christian message in Latin America is one of the inculturation of a foreign message. Popular Catholicism has its faults. The whole of the popular element — as must occur under a regime of domination — includes the dominator, with the result that elements of the nonpopular are found mingled with the popular. This inculturation, called popular Catholicism, has been a factor of resistance, and today, for the most part, constitutes a powerful force in the political liberation of our people.

A new evangelization, and hence a process of inculturation of the gospel, is spreading across the face of the continent. It is inspired by the commitment of our local and regional Latin American churches to take seriously, and not spiritualize, the preferential option for the poor. There is a new alliance between the hierarchy and the poor, the popular bases. From this alliance, an immense network of base communities has sprung. An authentic ecclesiogenesis is under way, giving birth to a new model of church, begotten of the faith of the people by the Spirit of God, amid a misery now no longer accepted, but rejected by a liberative understanding and practice. The church of the poor, also called the church of the "base" or grassroots, is a historico-social reality. It actualizes a different presence of the Christian message, amid the specific conditions of a Latin America in process of a "conscientization" (consciousness raising) with respect to its rampant inequalities and injustices, and with a view to transcending its oppressions.

The material object of liberation theology is this new practice on the part of the base church communities, this church of the poor. The new theological reflection reveals a new way of being Christian: the emergence of a new culture, built in a dialogue between faith and the people, between gospel and social justice. This new way of being Christian will make its contribution to the more comprehensive process now under way across the length and breadth of the Latin American continent.

4 | What Is the Gospel in Relation to Cultures and Religions?

The questions raised above with reference to evangelization in Latin America bring us back to a more basic question. When all is said and done, what is the gospel in relation to cultures and religions?

Let us begin with the more comprehensive of the pair: culture. As shown above, culture constitutes an absolutely primary datum. Everything human is cultural, at whatever level we take the human phenomenon. The human being lives in a culture as in house and home. In culture are developed the social and personal human reactions to the existential knots that structure human life: our relationship with subsistence goods, with ourselves, with others, with nature, with traditions, with the afterlife, and with God. Religion is one of the greatest, if not the greatest, of the creations of human culture. It is the vehicle of our deepest hopes, and the source of our most urgent questions. It patterns our management of the ultimate concepts bearing on salvation, eternal life, or perdition. Not without cause is religion so frequently invoked for the legitimation of power, as its imperatives are ultimate and without appeal. Every culture produces its religion—that is, organizes responses to the thirst for radicality and perpetuity in the human heart.

There are anthropological constants, always articulated differently, but ever-present, in all modulations: for instance, the need to organize the means of the production and reproduction of life (nutrition), the means of housing, of clothing, of communication (language and symbols), of work, of the ordering of sex roles, of social relations of work, of forms of power. One fundamental anthropological constant is the utopic faculty—the urge to project great dreams and to define the final framework of history and the world. The most archaic myths refer to these sorts of inquiries. The human being we know cannot but build a cultural elaboration on basic axes like these.

CULTURAL AND THEOLOGICAL MEANING OF RELIGIONS

Religion does more than attend to a desperate cry for help, or respond to the thirst for plenitude. This is merely the level of needs and wants. There is also the realm of gratuity. Human beings are also interested in the nature of that Being for whom they feel a call, and with whom they can freely enter into a relationship in service, thanksgiving, and confident surrender. Religions project a certain metaphysical content, expressed in the language of positivity or negativity, asserting plenitude and being, or void and nothingness, as human expressions of what is experienced as the most meaningful and relevant of all things: God, the Tao, Nirvana, and so forth.

This phenomenon deserves a theological reading. According to Christian theology, cultures, in their function of the production of meaning for life, in their ethical dimension, and especially in their religious expression, are an echo of the voice of God, who ever speaks to society and to every human subjectivity. Cultures are responses, more or less faithful, to God's proposal of communion, life, and fullness. Especially, religions are reactions to the antecedent action of God. They are manners in which God's self-communication to creatures is received. They are the conduit of God's revelation to humanity, in its differences of time, space, and cultural modulation.

The first eleven chapters of the Book of Genesis recall the permanent fact of God's revelation to all peoples, both yesterday and today. The Dogmatic Constitution *Dei Verbum* emphatically states: "God has manifested himself since the dawn of creation to our first fathers . . . watching over the human race in ongoing fashion" (no. 3). After all, "in many ways and at many times has God spoken to human beings" (Heb. 1:1).[19] Saint John is aware that the Word "enlightens everyone who comes into this world" (John 1:4). The Spirit ever inhabits the human world, filling our heart with enthusiasm for actions that generate life. In more radically theological terms: the Holy Trinity, that mystery of the communion of the three Divine Persons, is always engaged in self-bestowal on creation and on the life of every person, together with a self-revelation to human communities in the form of sociability, openness to others, love, and commitment, as well as denunciation of and protest at the absence of these values. All humanity is a temple of the Trinity, without distinction of time, place, or religion. All of us are sons and daughters in the Son, all are moved by the Spirit, all are drawn upward by the Father.

To this positivity, a negativity corresponds: the history of refusal, of self-centering to the point of the exclusion of others and of the calls of mystery. "Every human being is Adam, every human being is Christ," said Saint Augustine, with a fine perception of the contradictions of reality. Side by side with the celebration of meaning, then, is the perception of wickedness. The weeds pervade all the wheat, permanently and indissolubly.

By reason of this negative dialectic in humanity, we have the prophet, who denounces and dies a martyr, and the shepherd, who proclaims and animates all dimensions of light and life. Here too the Holy Trinity is revealed, *sub contrario*.

Cultures as a whole elaborate this complex, dramatic dialectic. They are the locus of a fervent acceptance of God's self-communication, as well as of a refusal of the same, or (most often of all) an ambiguous mixture of the two, which are never found pure. These two reactions are so inextricably intermingled that it becomes difficult to make an adequate judgment as to where the appeals of God are heeded and where they are ignored. Religion gathers up the diffuse responses of culture and codifies them, in rite, doctrine, symbols, and ethical codes. All religions, in this perspective of a basic theology, are responses to God's proposals. They are normal cultural routes to the divinity. They are also divine routes to cultures. God concretely encounters persons and societies "where they are" — in their actual organization in space and time. There God visits them in grace and forgiveness, in prophecy when they are in error, and in reward and munificence when they are correct and excellent.

This approach was communicated to the entire church by Vatican II. There the conciliar fathers helped us understand that revelation is not primarily a set of propositions to be regarded as true because God is their actual author. The council taught us that revelation is God's liberative deed in history, generating life in abundance and permitting the actual self-bestowal of God on the life of persons and all the divine creation (*Dei Verbum*). This conception opened the way for a positive appraisal of the history of humanity, a history steeped in grace and sin, but with the final victory guaranteed for grace (*Gaudium et Spes*). The religions, in the history of humanity, merit a highly positive consideration (*Nostra Aetate*). This evaluation lies at the basis of religious freedom, ecumenism, and the dialogue with the other religions (*Dignitatis Humanae*). The church must be understood as a sacrament of universal salvation—that is, as a sign and instrument of this salvation (*Lumen Gentium*), serving all humanity, especially those who suffer in their quests for life and redemption (*Gaudium et Spes*).

FOUR MEANINGS OF EVANGELIZATION

Against this background, what is meant by evangelization?

First, to evangelize means to bear testimony to this vision of respect and acceptance of all cultures on account of God and the divine work within cultures. The first missionary is the Holy Trinity, which, through the Logos and the Spirit, becomes present in every cultural fabric. Thus, all must engage in mutual evangelization, inasmuch as all must confront the signs wrought by God in all cultures, evaluating them, accepting them, admiring them, respecting them in their difference from our own, and entering into communion with them as one enters into communion with God. This first evangelization is possible only when what *Evangelii Nuntiandi* calls an "essential element, usually the first," which is "presence, participation, and solidarity" vis-à-vis the culture addressed by those who seek to evangelize (no. 21) has gone first. None evangelize without first committing themselves to life, to the productive forces of the culture they seek to reach with their evangelization. It is not enough to be merely "there": sheer presence in the culture. One must share that culture, discover life meanings in it, love it; and finally, be in solidarity with it. This is possible only through a process of identification with its advances and retreats, its potentials and its limitations.

Solidarity with a culture entails taking up the brilliance and splendor of that culture, as well as, critically, its dark side, for a culture is always a totality. There is no place here for the opportunistic attitude whereby one selects only what seems good to oneself (on what criteria?) and rejects what seems less so. To enter into solidarity with anyone is to become embodied in that person's culture, and to employ one's abilities and potential in assisting that culture to grow and blossom (the function of critical confrontation and creative practice, which constitute the permanent source of cultural creation). Only on the basis of this process of sympathy and empathy, as we learn from *Evangelii Nuntiandi* (no. 22), can there be any meaning in an evangelization that speaks of Christian positivity such as reign of God, incarnation, resurrection, divine filiation, and other content of the evangelical utopia.

This first point must not be regarded as mere "evangelical preparation"—that is, as a tactic for winning good will. It is the gospel itself, in the form of an atmosphere of benevolence, and of a discovery of the very presence of God in the various cultures. It is a spirituality, a mysticism, which sees to the heart of things, and discerns in cultural productions the human response to a divine proposal. The presence of this atmosphere is not only important, it is essential: it is a *conditio sine qua non* for the whole of explicit evangelization. Were the latter to be attempted without the mystique of the universal, dynamic presence of the triune God in the cultures, it would mean the imposition of theological content developed in the clothing of one culture and then superimposed on another, so-called evangelized culture. Without the gospel of fellowship, no message or practice can ever claim the title of evangelization. This viewpoint shows what was wrong with the "first evangelization" of Latin America, in the sixteenth century. It took place in a context not of fellowship but of conquest, domination, and destruction of the other.

Second, the religion of the culture being evangelized must be accepted theologically. Religion, as we know, and as has been stated above, is the soul of culture. Without a dialogue with its religion, no culture will ever be understood in its inward depths. The reading will always be extrinsic, and at bottom distorted, failing to do justice to the persons who experience the culture in question, or the deepest meaning they attach to their religion. In the familiar processes of evangelization, as long as the religion of the other was fought — indeed, destroyed — a process of cultural domination continued as well, entailing the imposition of an already inculturated Christianity. That is, evangelization as the self-generation of the gospel in terms of good news, from a point of departure in the cultural matrices of the other, was renounced.

Jesus' own practice was one of true evangelization. He felt himself to belong to the religion of his people. For him, holy scripture was the Old Testament, not the New. Jesus was not a Christian, but a Jew. Based on the faith experience of his people's tradition, he sought to convey to those around him his revelatory filial experience of his Father, an experience that acts in a transforming manner, in the power of the Spirit, in the history of the building up of the reign. In the words of Paul VI in *Evangelii Nuntiandi* (no. 7), Jesus was "the first evangelizer," and to evangelize is basically to do what Jesus did — proclaim a great hope, the reign, which starts out from the most utopic dimensions of the depths of the human heart: a creation finally rescued and delivered from all manner of oppression, in the joy of knowing God and being known by God.

The historical realization of this utopia entails the process of personal and collective change known as "conversion." This utopia is made known by concrete, anticipatory signs of a happy issue and consummation of all. One of the most convincing signs of this utopia is the constitution of a community that already experiences this novelty, amid the old world, witnessing to other persons the liberative signs from the various wants suffered by human beings in existence (disease, hunger, contempt for the poor who are now the first addressees of the gospel, and so forth), at the same time inviting others to become community. This pathway of evangelization bears the promise of a "renewal of humanity, giving rise to new men and women in a culture healed from its very roots" (cf. *Evangelii Nuntiandi*, nos. 7–17, 18–21).

Third, evangelization must produce, where it encounters cultures, that which its name proclaims: the good news. What is the good news? For whom is the good news good? There is no deciding beforehand what is good news without reference to specific cultures, and to the way these cultures deal with the basic expectancy of human existence. There is good reason for admitting the existence of a transcultural datum intrinsic to the various cultures, and bound up with the original meaning of life: the endorsement of life, and the desire for the perpetuity and full realization of the system of life. Human beings want to live, and live endlessly, not as a mere prolongation of life in their mortality, but as the actualization of all their potentials, which are expressed in desire, in libido, in utopias, and in hope against hope.

Death is the most difficult element to integrate, as it threatens the desire for unending life. What is the radical good news? It is to be able to hear, as promise and as realization, that there is life beyond death for each of us: there is an absolute realization of life as actualization of all its intrinsic potentials of being, communion, and communication. And this is what resurrection signifies.[20] Resurrection is much more than the resuscitation of a corpse. It is the fulfillment and realization of life in the delight of living. Good news, then, is resurrection.

Where is the positive element of Christianity? It consists in the assertion that this utopia (in the pregnant, positive sense of the word) entered history in the person of Jesus of Nazareth, who was born under Caesar Augustus and crucified under Pontius Pilate. This happy event is not only a datum in the biography of Jesus; it is an assertion with regard to all humanity that they are not to be cheated of their hope of life, but that they hope because resurrection is possible; and, finally, that the possible has already occurred, in someone actually of our nature. What is already present realization in Jesus is real promise for each human being. The human dough is permeated by a leaven—an anticipation of the new life already dwelling in our weary, old existence.

The kernel of the good news is the proclamation of the triumph of life, beginning with someone whose life was violently taken from him in an unjust crucifixion. The resurrection is not the pure and simple affirmation of life, as Nietzsche said it was: it is the transfiguration of life, from a starting point in life's historical defeat. This is a sign to us of the promise that the first heirs of the resurrection, after the unique case of Jesus, are to be those who share in Jesus' fate, those who have fallen in the struggle for justice and the cause of the life of the impoverished — those who have made their denunciations, struggled, and given their own lives. Jesus is the first of many brothers and sisters (cf. Rom. 8:29) who share in the resurrection.

Why did the resurrection occur with Jesus of Nazareth, and not with someone else, of some other age and clime? This question was of serious concern to the primitive Christian community. Scholars tell us that it was only in light of the resurrection that the christological process began to develop.[21] That is, the basic question was: Who is this Jesus, whom we know, in whose life we share, whose deeds we have beheld, at whose crucifixion we have stood in helplessness, and to whose resurrection we now bear this gladsome witness? How are we to understand this individual, thus transfigured? In order to give an adequate, exhaustive answer to this question (as adequate and exhaustive as possible), manifold titles were conferred on Jesus: prophet, rabbi, miracle worker, Son of David, messiah Christ, and others, and finally, Son of God, and very God incarnate in our wretchedness.

It is important to keep in mind that the goal of all these efforts of interpretation was to decipher who this Jesus is who was crucified and raised again, this bearer of new, full life. Accordingly, all deciphering of the mystery of Jesus (attained in its hidden reality, now revealed by the gradual discovery of the apostolic community) was for the purpose of grasping the radicality concealed in the resurrection event. At the term of the discovery process, the community could profess: Jesus of Nazareth, itinerant prophet, proclaimer of the reign, friend of the poor and outcast whom he treated as the first addressees of his message, critic of his time, revealer of God as parent whose child he felt himself to be, filled with charismatic strength (the Spirit), who liberated persons and invited them to a new relationship of genuine fellowship, who was rejected, crucified, and then raised again, could be no other than very God in our flesh. By him, the one we call God is present "absolutely"—present without remainder, let us say—present as complete self-bestowal, present to the point of being one of us. In virtue of the fact that we are his brothers and sisters, we, too, share in this new quality of existence in God. Rightly does Vatican II say: "By his incarnation, the Son of God in some sort joined himself to every human being" (*Gaudium et Spes*, no. 22). The Word was joined primarily to the human being Jesus. But as no human being can have an exhaustive capacity for God, we, too, his sisters and brothers, receive, in communion with him, this same capacity. Each of us is a virtual *assumptus homo venturus* ("assumed future human being").

We may call this series of insights, all of them centering on the resurrection event as explicitations and developments of that event, the gospel. To evangelize, then, means to bear witness to and to propose this great good fortune, and to attempt, in the company of others, to produce it. As we see, the gospel bears on the destiny of all life, and on the ultimate meaning of history. It is opposed to no culture. On the contrary, it welcomes the most fundamental, generative power of culture, which is the desire for life (in the economic area, the political, the symbolical, the religious, and so on) present in all cultures.

Finally, to evangelize is also to *celebrate*. It is of the essence of Christianity to celebrate, throughout the warp and woof of life, the presence of the one who was raised. Particularly important, in this sense, is the eucharistic celebration. Here, primary elements of our Mediterranean culture—bread and wine—signify new life, already actual in the figure of Jesus and now open to being shared by all. In other cultures it will be other elements (rice in Asian cultures, maize in central American, and so on) that will serve as the symbolical basis for signaling the presence of risen life here and now, in our very history. Resurrection, although concentrated in the eucharistic celebration, is not restricted to it. It points to a process of transformation of the old life into the new, a transformation that pervades all processes, up to and including the ultimate transfiguration of the universe, in its own resurrection.

Each culture expresses this realized utopia, rooting it in the furthest depths of our myths, in the most primitive throbbings of our unconscious, and in the most radical quests of every heart. Thus, this utopia is part and parcel of the potential of every cultural language. Our Western culture has used the tools of various cultural traditions (Jewish, Greek, Roman, Germanic, modern) to utter the resurrection event and all that it implies. But it does not pretend to have exhausted that event, or deciphered its mystery.

5 | Cultures Assimilate the Gospel

Evangelization cannot occur apart from culture. Evangelization always arrives astride existing cultural worldviews. The gospel is not identified *with* cultures, but it is identified *in* cultures, unable ever to exist apart from a cultural expression, be it the one articulated by Jesus in the Semitic universe, or by Paul within the parameters of Hellenism and the Judaism of the diaspora, or by the Christians of the first centuries in the matrices of Greco-Roman, and later, barbarian, culture.

Puebla was correct, then:

> The faith transmitted by the Church is lived out on the basis of a presupposed culture. In other words, it is lived by believers who are deeply attached to a culture, and hence "the construction of the kingdom cannot help but take over elements from human culture and cultures." [Puebla Final Document, no. 400; citing *Evangelii Nuntiandi*, no. 20]

As previously agreed, every culture, simply by being a culture, is a response (positive, negative, ambiguous) to God's proposal. Inescapably, then, in every culture there will be buds, shoots of the reign, sacraments of grace, signs of the presence of the Word, and accents of the activity of the Spirit. In every culture, the Old and New Testaments coexist. The divine Trinity is already dynamically acting in the cultural processes — engaged in a gradual process of self-bestowal (this would be the Old Testament) and finally giving itself in its totality, without any intermediation, to the whole of humanity, to every human being, man and woman, all represented concretely in Jesus of Nazareth (the New Testament). The decisive element is not in Jesus' being a male, a Jew of Galilee, a member of a Mediterranean culture based on wheat, olive oil, and wine (the primordial elements of the reproduction of life and culture there). The decisive element is Jesus' vicarious presentation of the whole of humanity (which is realized in every human being and in different cultural ways) as assumed by the divinity — or an entire humanity receiving the whole of the divinity. The assertion of the reality of this event constitutes the Christian positivity to be offered to the free acceptance of all human beings in their ways of organizing and reproducing life.

What concrete echoes such a proclamation can awaken in various cultures is a matter for case-by-case verification. We know of few inculturations of this gospel. The Hebrew, the Greek, the Roman, the Germanic, and the modern inculturations are the only ones. As for the reception of this gospel in the Guarani, Nahuatl, Maya, Quechua, Yoruba, or Xavante culture, this will depend on these cultures. We do not know what would emerge. It seems clear today that to evangelize is not to reproduce one's own cultural expression in another person. Evangelization cannot be an adaptation of the gospel to the superficial dimensions of culture. It must, as Paul VI insisted, plunge "to the depths" of culture, "to its very roots" (*Evangelii Nuntiandi*, no. 20): evangelization must produce the gospel culturally as good news, must be a self-generation of the gospel in the form of a comprehensive, ultimate meaning of a cultural whole. Faith, in this creative process, is more a mystique of encounter with the divinity than the appropriation of a creed: it is experienced rather as a spirituality than as a dogmatics.[22] Why? Because it is not so much the gospel that is inculturated, as culture that, after its own fashion, incorporates the gospel.

We hear that the gospel must be inculturated. That is, it must penetrate to the roots of a culture, and thus actually take on the expressions of that culture. This familiar jargon suggests that there is such a thing as a gospel-in-itself, endowed with an intrinsic power to fertilize the various cultures. Actually, this is not the case. The gospel is never naked. It is always culturally clothed. The fact that revelation and the gospel have been codified in Western Jewish and Christian cultures, and that the Bible is the inspired book (it remains to define precisely in what dogmatic sense this should be taken) does not mean that its cultural expression participates in the irreformable essence of the gospel and revelation. We must say that every cultural expression not only assumes the gospel, but restricts it as well. It concretizes it, but it limits it as well. This assertion is an important one. Unless we appreciate this fact, we risk taking the cultural version of the Christian faith in its Western matrices, in which the creed, our dogmas, and our theology have been enfleshed, as pertaining essentially to the gospel itself. Indeed, historically evangelization has meant an implantation of Western culture, whether in China, Latin America, or Africa.

REDUCTIVE ASSIMILATION OF CHRISTIANITY

Even a cursory comparison of the biblical inculturation of the gospel with its Greco-Romano-Germanic inculturation will demonstrate that an enormous process of assimilation occurred—an assimiliation that, on today's criteria, we should have to call reductive. Let us look at some examples.

Concept of God. Biblically, God is conceptualized in categories of life and history, covenant with humanity, and ethic of justice and solidarity with the wronged. In the Western inculturation, God was represented in terms of the metaphysics of being: as the supreme Being, immobile, immutable, and suprahistorical. Faith in the triune God, Father, Son, and Spirit, was inculturated as faith in God the divine nature, all-powerful, all-wise, and all-provident.

The *figure of the reign* is a holistic, political category. Biblically it signifies the totality of creation redeemed and organized on the criteria of God's loving design. The reign represents the comprehensive politics of God, to be implemented in the history of the cosmos, of nations, of the chosen people, and in the depths of each human heart. In the Western inculturation, the reign was transformed into a synonym for the other world, the afterlife. It suffered a profound spiritualization, and complete depoliticization. This error is all the more serious in that we know that the reign constitutes the *ipsissima intentio Jesu*, the original proposition of the historical Jesus.

Perception of history. Biblically, history is the great reality in which God's revelation is wrought and the divine design realized. It is a process, and moves toward an eschatological plenitude to be attained in an onerous dialectic of confrontation, failure, mercy, and the triumph of life and God. For the inculturation of the gospel in the Greco-Roman universe, history is irrelevant. It adds nothing new, since events are accidents of an essence ever identical with itself, or fleeting apparitions of a project eternally defined by God. This attitude leads to an utter secularization of history. History is now theologically irrelevant. This is why Christians (especially the hierarchy) have interfered in it without serious ethical scruples, or any inspiration drawn from faith: history is of no definitive account.

Concept of the human being. Biblically, the human being is represented as a unit of existential situations, in flesh, body, and spirit. Every basic situation shapes a project. The project of the flesh is a project earthly and of earth, that of a self-actualization in total selfishness. The project of the body bears upon the person, social and individual, and is always open to communion with others. The dimensions of the project of the spirit open out upon the divine transcendency, in the perspective of a blessed, joyous life in and with God. In the Greco-Roman inculturation, the human being was viewed as a composition of two "principles," body and soul, with all real value concentrated in the soul: the body was only a burden, from which we must be delivered in a thousand ways. The future belongs to the soul alone. It is in the soul that God dwells. And the pastoral ministry is the care of souls. The body is left to itself, subjected, chastised, and given over to the grave.

Message of resurrection. Biblically, the promise of the resurrection is the human being's utter fulfillment, external and internal. The resurrection is the great utopia of the new man and woman—good news to be realized, starting with Jesus, in all persons, even in this world, and culminating in the gladsome encounter with God in the afterlife. In the inculturation of the faith in Western culture, the resurrection was relegated to the "end of the world." It lost its whole evangelizing appeal, since it was no longer promised for this time, as an expression of our participation in Jesus raised. It was more and more absorbed into the Platonic doctrine of the immortal soul, which by death is delivered from the prison of this corruptible body. Only then does the soul live, free, in God. Only at the term of history would it be reunited with the body, which has dissolved in matter. Thus, the fundamental unity of the human being is destroyed, and the resurrection is partialized, since it reaches the body alone, while the soul is immortal by nature.

These are only examples. My purpose here is not to oppose one inculturation to another, the Jewish to the Western. But inculturations utter and conceal, assert and limit. What I wish to emphasize is the risk of fusing the gospel with its instruments of inculturation, and coming to regard the gospel as merely cultural—and on this account imposing one culture on another, thus preventing the latter from making its own assimilation of the gospel, with the same right and freedom as the Jewish, Greco-Roman, and Germanic cultures did so.

Nor do I wish to assert the superiority of one inculturation over another. Inculturations are merely different. Each produces a meaning whole. What must not be allowed to make its appearance is a monopoly of the experience of the gospel. All cultures can and should make their own syntheses, on an equal footing, as the fruit of a process of assimilation in the frameworks of their respective matrices. All must produce the good news of life.

By this I mean that the ongoing, fundamental datum is culture. Culture is already impregnated with revelation, gospel, and God. When its social actors place it in contact with the positivity of faith and the gospel (as revelation of the absolute affirmation of life by resurrection, and all that this implies in terms of God, divine filiation, activity of the Spirit in history, and so on), culture assimilates this as it can, and expresses it in the available codes of its totality.

This process is dialectical, and calls for a twofold osmosis: the culture is transfigured in contact with the gospel, and the gospel is inculturated in relation to the cultural matrices. But this dialectic establishes its relation from the cultural pole: the *analogatum princeps*, the governing analogue, is culture. It is from here that the gospel exists as a historical reality. Once inculturated, the gospel impinges on other cultures, once again to undergo a process of sifting and osmosis as it is received into the roots of another culture.

All of this must also be conceived in its negative dialectic, of negation, ambiguity, insufficiency, and distortion. But these pathologies are possible only given the basic healthiness of the whole inculturation. Only a healthy body can become diseased; and any disease bespeaks a reference to a health to be recovered and preserved.

Concretely, in the process of evangelization we see the encounter of a previously inculturated gospel with another culture (in its social actors) with which it has not yet been confronted, and which therefore has obviously not assimilated it. Here we must be attentive to two phenomena.

The first is that, in the concrete, there is no such thing as a meeting of cultures. The meeting is always between social actors of two or more distinct cultures. For example, the "twelve apostles" (the first Franciscan missionaries in Mexico, beginning in 1521) conduct an arduous dialogue with the Aztec sages. In the course of the dialogue, the cultural structures of both partners emerge: their respective languages, customs, worldviews, religions, their way of understanding power and of defining the meaning of mutual presence: as conquest, as military and religious invasion. In this mutual encounter of social actors (against a background of the activity of cultural structures) a certain imponderable emerges: human practice, a capacity to engage in dialogue in such a way as to produce something new, something that transcends cultural conditions. This is the specificity of human practice: to be creative of the new, and not merely reproductive of the old. This new element is the fruit of the encounter of actors, of their specific horizons, and of the problem-posing that emerges in confrontation with others. It is on the basis of this phenomenon that the gospel, as utopia, as radically human summons and call, can be grasped in transcendence of its specific inculturation, and assimilated (or rejected) by another culture.

The second phenomenon is the following. In order for dialogue and encounter to take place, a "field of communion" is necessary—a common ground that is broader than either of the cultures in confrontation. Every human being is a cultural being. No human being exists apart from a cultural determination. But human beings, precisely in their quality as human, are transcultural as well. That is, the essence of the human being cannot be exhaustively represented in any determinate cultural articulation. Each culture explicitates and organizes human virtualities, but leaves just as many others unrealized and concealed, to be explicitated by other cultures. For example, science and technology, in their origin, are expressions of Western culture. But the science and technology that are spreading throughout the world today are not only Western; they are human. In their quality as human, they can be understood and assumed by other human beings, of East and West, including members of the original societies of various parts of the world. This is why we can learn from the old Chinese, Japanese, and Grecian sages, or appreciate Egyptian, Mayan, and Aztec poetry. Besides being what they are in their cultural specificity, these things are human, and open to being understood and grasped by human beings everywhere. It is somewhat the same with the gospel. The gospel can be assimilated by different cultures, and reveal different intrinsic virtualities, as it is incorporated into the cultural matrices of various peoples. But it is always open to new inculturations.

PARADIGMS OF AN INTEGRAL EVANGELIZATION

In the process of evangelization we discern five fundamental paradigms.

The first is the *incarnation* paradigm. The culture allows the gospel to become incarnate in its matrices. The process is one of "assumption,"[23] and entails the limitations of any assumption. But it is only thus, in limitation, that the gospel becomes concrete. Every culture is somehow an absolute—or better, a concrete universal. It constitutes a system of complete meaning.

The second paradigm is the *Trinity* paradigm: the fundamental relationality of all cultures. True, the latter are all complete systems. But these systems are open to other systems and cultures, since no culture exhausts the potential of the personal and social human being. Among the cultures there should prevail what prevails in the trinitarian mystery—the radical relationality among the three divine Persons. Each is one and irreducible; and yet each stands ever in relationship and perichoresis with the others. The communion and reciprocity of the divine Persons makes them one God. A respect, as it were, for this relationality precludes the domination of one divine Person by another. This same structure of relationality ought to prevail among cultures, as well.

The third paradigm is the *redemption* paradigm. Incarnation and relationality set the cultures in mutual confrontation not only in their essence and health, but in their distortions and pathologies as well. Redemption accomplished in dialogue and intercultural confrontation necessarily entails an awareness of imperfection, mistakes, and errors in cultures. No one is a criterion for anyone else. However, each cultural totalization should be required to show to what extent it produces life for all, especially for the poor and the outcast—show to what point it enhances personal freedom. Such values are the foundations of humanity; and they are transcultural criteria for an appraisal of the level of hominization and humanization, or lack thereof, promoted by the various cultures.

The fourth is the *resurrection* paradigm. All cultures, especially when enriched through a dialogue with persons and groups of other cultures, are summoned and impelled to a transfiguration—to an ongoing openness, and to the exploitation of all of the possibilities latent in their matrices. Each culture ought to permit itself creativity, which means the irruption of the new, in anticipation of an absolute transparency in intersubjective relations and in social communications. The resurrection principle postulates the full realization of the possibilities inherent in the cultural matrices, finally pointing to an absolute transhistorical meaning, whose anticipations and concrete signs these realized possibilities feel themselves to be.[24]

Finally, there is the *reign* paradigm. The reign paradigm denotes the ultimate framework of all cultures. All cultures, like all peoples, belong to the reign of the Trinity. They will not disappear. We do not know how or when the purifying judgment and transfiguration of each culture will occur. We know that cultures will always exist, wherever human beings are present, since the human race is inconceivable without culture. Cultures will share in the happy consummation of humanity—in its full insertion into the trinitarian life, where God will be all in all cultures.

6 | Christian Obstacles to the Inculturation of the Gospel Today

There are all kinds of obstacles to the inculturation of the gospel: rigidity in cultures themselves, which are so arrogant in their traditions and historical role and incapable of a self-interrogation in depth; structures of injustice, which render persons and institutions insensitive to the cries of the oppressed; the insolence of persons who refuse dialogue, and close themselves in on their own cultural values; and so forth. Here I want to concentrate on one point only: historical Christianity itself as one of the obstacles to the inculturation of the gospel.

Undeniably, the gospel in history launched a fantastic torrent of generosity and selfless service to others — a true marvel of the exaltation of human dignity. It produced figures of the highest anthropological significance, by any criteria of past or present: Saint Francis of Assisi, Bartolomé de Las Casas, Albert Schweitzer, Martin Luther King, Jr., Dom Hélder Câmara, and so on. Undeniably, it produced culture, and a culture expressed in the depths of human existence precisely as human, and hence universal. Any analyst, even one not professing the Christian faith, must acknowledge all of this.

But especially in its Roman Catholic version, Christianity has left a counterbalance of negatives that must not be ignored. In the intercultural dialogue of today it manifests painful limitations. These are due especially to the image it projects to others, to non-Christians who must undergo, who must suffer, our evangelization process. It is also due to the way in which it is organized internally. Let me examine each of these two points.

CHRISTIANITY AS SEEN BY THE NONPROFESSING

If one looks at Christianity historically, from the viewpoint of those who do not profess it, the image it presents is that of a religion, a product of Western culture, with all manner of short-comings, especially in its claim to be the only true religion, to hold the monopoly on revelation and salvation. The West today seems more and more a traumatic accident in overall human progress. Why? Because it has been in the Christian West that the great ideologies and practices of world domination have been generated: the Enlightenment, capitalism, and Leninist-Stalinist communism. It has been the Christian West that has promoted colonialism, and the subjugation of the cultures of Asia, Africa, and Latin America. In this process of military invasion, commercial occupation, political tyranny, and ideological domination, genocide has been committed that have no precedent in the history of humanity. The language most used has been that of harsh violence, repression of resistance, and extinction of yearnings for liberty. With rare exceptions, the West has satanized the religions of others,[25] and thus opened the way for their destruction or permanent persecution.

Many martyrs of Catholicism are not really such in the strict sense. They died because they had manifested, with the harshest expressions and the most insolent deeds, a contempt for the religions, rites, and deities of other peoples. These peoples then defended themselves by eliminating their assailants. The expansion of the European ecclesiastical system to other parts of the world was generally accompanied by the paraphernalia of military power and social privilege. It was not difficult for this solid power bloc to subject colonial peoples. How can one not understand the language of the subjected Indians who complained that the god of the Christians was cruel, unjust, and ruthless? Until the very day of judgment, the descendants of the blacks shipped over from Africa to be scattered across various countries of this continent like beasts of burden will have the right to indemnification in terms of justice and humanity from the Christian whites who enslaved them to use as cheap fuel for the production of their filthy lucre.

Despite this ugly scar on the history of a Christianity that is Western and accidental in its language, its manner, its rites, and its thought — at the same time it is this Western, historical Christianity that is partly responsible for the scientific and techno-logical project of modernity we see creating the authentic transcultural ecumenism that surrounds us today. Today we have the power to defeat archenemies of humanity like hunger, endemic diseases, distance, and violent forces of nature. Science and technology have enabled us to create the conveniences of modern human existence, thereby lightening the burden of mortal life. At the same time, modern science and technology have become the most effective weapon for the harnessing of the peoples maintained in underdevelopment, peoples bled dry by the prices they must pay for technological formulas and scientific projects. On this point Christianity has been perhaps too little negative — not critical enough to appreciate the huge potential for domestication, uniformization, and westernization transferred to other cultures from the central countries of the social, political, and cultural order of the West, which holds the hegemony in world politics. The link between Christianity and the ideology and practice of Western domination produces a cloud of ambiguity and complicity, enormously tarnishing the brilliance of the evangelical practice and utterance of Jesus.

CHRISTIANITY AS SEEN BY THOSE WHO PROFESS IT

Another reason for the difficulty of inculturating the gospel in cultures today is the way the institutional dimension of the Roman Catholic Church is organized. The church of Christ understands itself as a sacramental mystery — that is, as a reality bearing on the most fundamental divine realities, such as the Holy Trinity, the definitive salvation of creation, and the resurrection of the dead (its mystery side), as well as on sociohistorical realities like insertion into a particular culture, which insertion entails the power and frailty of the human condition and therefore inconsistencies and sins (its sacramental side). To be sure, the total church (mystery and sacrament, hierarchy and faithful) lives what the creed professes: it is one, holy, catholic, and apostolic. But these theological realities are realized in contradiction: the moral deficiencies and historical limitations common to humankind persist. The path taken by the church in Western culture, for example, defines its current institutional profile. Every historical stage has left its marks on the social fabric of the church: the imperial Roman culture, the feudal, the aristocratic, the capitalistic, the modern, and the popular.

Western culture has always been marked by the logocentrism and individualism of the Greek tradition. By contrast, primitive Christianity was profoundly communitarian. Then, through the process of its inculturation, it allowed itself to be impregnated with interiorism. The ancient and medieval world of the West, until the appearance of the representative republic (beginning with the French Revolution), was predominantly authoritarian and "centralistic" in terms of the exercise of power. In the church, besides the spirit of participatory democracy found in almost all forms of religious life, there is also a centralized form of government, wielded by the Roman curia and the power amassed by the papacy. This all but founders under the weight of the decisions attributed to it. Decentralization, and more thoroughgoing actualization of the principle of collegiality of bishops and the national and continental bishops' conferences would facilitate a differentiated inculturation of the gospel in the various regions of the world of today.

The official liturgy of the church is strongly marked by the Western experience of a perceived superiority of spirit to matter, a mistrust of the body and its passions, and great restraint in its symbolic expression. Non-Western cultures, such as those of Africa and Latin America, esteem the human totality, especially its bodily nature, and express this esteem in their material symbolism—in dance, for instance. These cultures are perplexed when, in the process of evangelization, they assist at sacramental rites and the eucharistic celebration. Very often, certain colors and certain animals have diametrically opposite meanings from those acquired in Western culture. For example, in China the color of joy is black, and ought to be used on Easter Sunday instead of on Good Friday; again in China, the dragon, which for us Westerners represents the Evil One, signifies heavenly protection. To display an image of Our Lady crushing the head of a dragon, and not explain what this is intended to mean, is to affront the most basic values of Chinese culture.

The most conscious groups of the "witness cultures" of Latin America (the Mayas, the Aztecs, the Incas, the Quechuas, and so on) have not forgotten what the Iberian colonists, Christians all, perpetrated upon the native populations. What the pontifical commission *Justitia et Pax* declared in its document of November 8, 1988, "The Church and Racism," is scarcely to be denied:

> The first great wave of European colonization [in the New World] was indeed accompanied by the massive destruction of the pre-Columbian civilizations, and a brutal subjugation of their populations. If the great navigators of the fifteenth and sixteenth centuries were without racist preconceptions, the soldiers and merchants were less respectful. They killed in order to take control. In order to take advantage of the labor of the "natives," and then the blacks, they reduced them to slavery, and began to develop a racist theory to justify themselves. [no. 3]

Deeds of this kind, perpetrated in contravention of the spirit of Christianity, soiled the image of the institutional church, which for the rest, in venerable missionary and episcopal figures, defended with all its might the dignity of the natives against the abuses of colonists.

Generally speaking, for the modern mentality, the Western version of Christianity has done precious little to integrate human subjectivity, affectivity, corporality, femininity, and the more open and effective mechanisms of participation in decisions as to the pathways to be taken by the faith in the various situations of life. The laity could have a greater voice, women could be more highly regarded for their consultative and decision-making capacities, and dialogue could be broader in all areas of church life. Then the claim of the church to be a "specialist in humanity," and Jesus' utopic "you are all my brothers and sisters" (cf. Matt. 21:8) would sound less like rhetoric and more like ongoing practice.

7 | The Need for the Church
To Be Evangelized
by Cultures

The preceding chapter explained the challenge of Paul VI: "The Church stands ever in need of evangelization" (*Evangelii Nuntiandi*, no. 15). But who is to evangelize the church — especially its governing body, the hierarchy?

In the first place, Puebla gives us a precious indication when it recognizes the evangelizing potential of the *poor*, who "challenge the church constantly, calling it to conversion" (Puebla Final Document, no. 1147). Indeed it is the poor who today most evangelize the theologians, priests, religious, and bishops. They evangelize by what is proper to them, and what was grasped so well by the whole Old Testament: by their outcry against injustice, their demand for liberation, by the call for solidarity provoked by their misery, by their will to participation, that they may be the agents of their history and of their church community. They have helped the hierarchy make a preferential option for the poor. Before the bishops expressed this evangelical option, the poor had made an option for the church. Indeed, the church (as an institutional whole) had for many years been a powerful advocate of their demands, and offered them a social space (as well as, at times, a physical one) in which to associate and discuss their problems. We must never forget that they, the poor, are the heirs of the first beatitude, and of the hope awakened by Jesus for a reconciled world of justice, the sign of the reign in history. Amid their wretchedness, they have not lost sight of the basic values of Jesus' utopia: solidarity, sharing, fellowship, historical patience, faith in providence, and hope against hope. These realities are the food of Christian existence. This is the experience of the poor who evangelize the hierarchy and all other Christians who have not lost a sense of observation and a sensitivity to evangelical values.

In the second place, besides the poor, the church has much to learn, as Vatican II says, "from the *history of the development of humanity*" (*Gaudium et Spes*, no. 44). In all cultures, there are true, divine elements, the fruit of the action of the world and the activity of the Holy Spirit. In principle, the church has always been open to such contributions. But it has also been oblivious of the difficulties springing from its own Western inculturation, difficulties in distinguishing between what is cultural and what is an irreformable datum of God's revelation. And here, generally speaking, it has been more prudent than courageous—more loyal to its own experience than to a necessary openness to new efforts at inculturation.

A notorious conflict persists between the church (especially in its ordinary magisterium) and modern culture. This has not arisen altogether independently of Christian ideas (autonomy of the religious vis-à-vis the political, secularization, dignity of the human person, and so forth). As it happens, however, the emancipation movements of modernity have had to take a critical position with regard to sectors of the hierarchy that, for historical reasons, had forged ties with the old feudal and aristocratic order. To defend its privileges, it excluded and oppressed the new, emerging forces.

The idea of democracy (power originating with the people and transmitted to their representatives and controlled by law) is difficult to assimilate in some circles: truth, we are told, is not a matter to be determined by majority vote. But this is not the point of a democracy. The point of a democracy is a universal share in the exercise and control of power. Truth, even the truth of power, is not a matter of majority vote. Truth has its own consistency, independent of minority or majority opinions. Jesus was a minority, and died in isolation. Yet the truth was with him, and not with the majority, the priests and the people. All of this we know.

Further: the inflation of modern subjectivity, the relativization of basic values, which open the way for every kind of permissiveness offending against right and justice, and a reluctance to admit an authentic transcendence that would relativize, and thereby hamper, historical absolutisms—positions maintained by modern culture—show us why the magisterium of the church keeps a critical distance from modernity. But this does not justify the attitude, encountered in certain more conservative ecclesiastical circles (Lefebvre was its foremost exponent), that the world is something decadent and distressing, and chiefly meriting mistrust and systematic suspicion. This would be a lack of faith in the presence of God in our history, too. This kind of pessimism leads to a projection of the concept of the church as the sole depository of truth, incapable of learning from the truths aroused by the Spirit in other human processes.[26]

Modern culture, despite its will to power, has accustomed us to criticism, to dialogue, as a way of learning from others and enriching our store of human and divine truth. We have become accustomed to recognizing our errors, and to the learning process these errors can set afoot. Modern scientists and scholars furnish us with examples of humility—of awareness of the fact that there is more ignorance than knowledge (even in theology), more challenges to be met than certitudes to be defended at all cost. Theologians and the doctrinal authorities of the church ought to imitate them. Were they to adopt similar attitudes, their pronouncements would be more likely to be heard and accepted by reasonable persons of our culture (who thus would open themselves more readily to the liberating truth of the gospel), than with their claim to be in a position to teach the whole world, and the atmosphere of arrogance that surrounds them. The gospel is more clearly manifest in an attitude of humility than in one of pomposity.

Democratic modernity has taught us tolerance. This is a fundamental attitude for evangelization. Tolerance is not the attitude of those who respect others because they cannot be rid of them. It is the attitude of those who are delighted to receive others because they realize that they have need of them and their experiences in order the better to grasp the truth of the world, humankind, and God. Had there been this kind of tolerance in the evangelization of Latin America, and the evangelization of modern understanding, we should not have fallen, as Christians, into so many mistakes, condemning what we later had to incorporate as human values and consequences of the very gospel. Christianity would have had a more mestizo profile in Latin America, and more participatory, democratic dimensions in modern culture.

There is a unmeasurable difference between Pius IX's "Syllabus of Errors" (1864), with its severe, condemnatory tone, and Vatican II's *Gaudium et Spes* a century later (1968), with its perspective of dialogue and acceptance of the good fruits of modern culture springing from work, science, and technology. In the interim, the church clearly underwent a necessary learning process.

Finally, the Roman Catholic Church can be evangelized by the rest of the Christian *churches*, and by the *religions* of the world. The legacy of Jesus, by virtue of its character of mystery, cannot be totally expressed in a single historico-social articulation, however excellent that articulation may be. It is like what happened with the gospel. The gospel is one, of course, and it is Jesus himself. But it is attested by four writings called Gospels. Each of these Gospels tells "the whole story," but each tells it from a point of departure in a different theological interest. We all regret the divisions in the one church of Christ, which have given rise to distinct Christian churches. And notwithstanding, each church possesses its evangelical values, which enrich the overall phenomenon of Christianity in history. The Roman Catholic Church has much to learn from the Protestant churches where love of the word of God is concerned. It has much to learn from the Orthodox churches where attention to the liturgy and the symbolic life of faith is concerned. From the Pentecostal churches it can learn inculturation in popular culture, and creativity in the organization of its various services and ministries.

The religions of the world, especially those of the Far East, teach us mysticism as a popular movement, a passion for transcendence, the unification of adoration with daily life, and the quest for an integration of the human being with the presence of mystery in all things.

The gospel does not have its first beginnings only in the historical Jesus. The eternal Logos and the Spirit have always been and still are at work in the world, leavening the dough of history with the yeast of the gospel of the Father, throughout the process of a creation that rises to the definitive reign of the Trinity. It is by associating itself with this gospel, a gospel sown clear across the historical process, that the Roman Catholic Church is evangelized, and becomes more authentically catholic.

8 | Challenges to Evangelization from Cultures in Latin America

The basic question of this chapter is the perspective from which cultures of Latin America ought to be evangelized. It is here that the outlook of liberation comes into play — not out of any ideological consideration, but in response to the challenges of the oppressed reality of this continent and of the world.

SEEN FROM BELOW: FROM CULTURES OF THE OPPRESSED AND OUTCAST

It is superfluous to observe that life and freedom throughout the world are altogether precarious. Some live in abundance, but at the cost of the almost absolute misery of the great population majorities of the earth. On one side we see the emergence of great cultural processes nearly everywhere; on the other side, entire cultures are threatened with annihilation, or else crushed to the point of silence — the cultures of the populations of the poor, whose access to the means of the maintenance and promotion of life is withheld.

In this context, the perspective of liberation gains great relevance. For Christians (of whatever confession), the only responsible alternative is: to make their faith a force for liberation, and a factor of criticism of an established order so perverse and inhumane for so many millions. The crucial question is not how to save Christianity, but how to save humanity and all the ecosystems threatened with new forms of apocalypse. This time there will be no Noah's ark to rescue the few from the deadly fate of the many. This time we shall all be swallowed up in the same cataclysm. The question is not how and in what form Christianity can be equal to, can respond to, these universal challenges, but how Christianity, along with other agencies, can help preserve the sacred gift of life. It can do so if it adopts, consciously, a libertarian perspective, and with regard to the whole problem, rather than its own confessional interests.

To put the fundamental question in this way is to require a shift in both the accent and the items of the theological agenda. Today more than ever before, what is needed is a theological cosmology. The great mystery, after that of the triune God, is the mystery of the world, that *sine qua non* of the divine self-communication, of the incarnation, the coming of the Spirit, and salvation history. And when I say world, I mean not only the complex of created beings, but also the series of social and political relationships that have arisen in history. The world has an eternal destiny. It is the world that is destined to be the body of the Trinity in trinitarian, cosmological, personal, and historico-social dimensions. Within the world is the church, with its mission of anticipating the happy lot of creation and of helping to bring that end about in all its dimensions. Liberation must be conceived not as being for the poor alone, but as being for all, beginning with the very poorest and in the universalistic outlook of the poor.

Taking the situation in Latin America, we see the following picture, in broad strokes: we have the cultures of domination, mimetism, resistance, and liberation.

The *culture of domination* characterizes all Latin America. It reveals the presence of foreign powers in our territory, with their imported languages, their imported science and technology, their imported customs, imported values, and even their way of organizing Christianity, which is Roman or Western. The culture of domination represents ongoing violence, because it is superimposed on the cultures already here, obliging them to restructure themselves, and, in large part, to dissolve. Latin American Indians feel like strangers in their own home, where the conqueror has climbed in through the windows and expelled those who lived there, or attacked and murdered them. The dominating culture has its center far from our continent: with a few years' lag, it has introduced its variations into all the countries of Latin America. It has not only its foreign agents, but its domestic allies as well, whom it adopts as its own.

We also have the *culture of mimesis*, produced by the governing elite. This elite does not produce an original culture, but imitates the culture of others. It does not create, it mimics — adapts without creativity. The culture of the national dominating groups is a consumer culture, and those who forge it are spectators of the history of others, not subjects or agents of their own history and that of the people, of whom they are ashamed.

Both the culture of domination and the culture of mimetism are alienated cultures, without roots in Latin American social reality. But both cultures readily perpetuate themselves, since they manage to introject themselves into the mentalities of the dominated, thus ensuring their submission from within. The dominating culture finds its correlative in the dominated culture (and this is why it is dominated) suffered by the people. A great part of popular culture is a reflex of the culture of the elite, adopted by the people in the course of the process of domination and adjustment to domination. Thus, many antipopular elements prevail in popular culture, and these inauthentic elements always need to be distinguished from the authentic ones, which actually translate the people's life and struggles.

There is the *culture of resistance* maintained by the oppressed. This is the effort exerted by exploited laborers, blacks, Indians, and women to resist the strategy of domination of the national and transnational governing classes. Generally speaking, the culture of resistance is characterized by a profound ambiguity. On the one hand it preserves the characteristics of the culture of the dominated, thereby guaranteeing its own identity, rebuilding hope, and maintaining in the people a sense of being alive. Here it is authentic, although it has precious little opportunity for independent development. On the other hand, it assumes the characteristics of the dominating culture — giving these characteristics, however, another meaning, under the appearances of adherence to and reproduction of the dominating culture. Especially, black culture and popular Catholicism, both charged with the symbolism of the dominating religion (but endowing it with a different content), represent religions of resistance.

Finally, there is the *culture of liberation*. This is the culture of the dominated groups that have become conscious of their domination — that therefore organize in movements where they gather strength, and immediately attempt practices that create freedom and alternatives to the established order of domination. Everywhere in Latin America — in tenant associations, in unions, in religious communities, and in certain political parties of popular, democratic extraction — we are witnessing the sudden appearance of a culture of liberation. It has its symbols, its hymns, its historical references, its martyrs, its language, and especially its organizational force. It is here that the originality of Latin American culture is being developed.

If we are to evangelize cultures, we must be clear as to where we start from: the cultures of resistance and liberation, whose strength will be enhanced by an evangelization of criticism, denunciation, and historical transcendence of the cultures of domination and mimetism. The alienated cultures of the dominating and mimetistic groups are evangelized only if they cease to be what they are — that is, if their dominating character is destroyed. This is what evangelical conversion means for the dominating cultures. What will remain of them when there is no more domination? They will be toppled from their thrones, surprised to find themselves elbow to elbow with the cultures of the people. Now they will be able to strike a solidarity with these cultures. The dominating cultures, which incorporate the values, knowledge, and technologies of the centers of foreign domination, must review and revise all of this alienated content of theirs, bringing it into the service of the promotion of popular power. It is the popular culture that must lead, and come to create the conditions necessary for its hegemony within the nation.

An evangelization that starts from the dominated cultures (the cultures of resistance and liberation) will validate the entire transformatory potential of those cultures, performing a function of criticism, and thereby assisting in the rejection of the dominator, who also acts within these cultures. Thus, evangelization will be associating itself with the quests and struggles of these cultures. Faith, too, will make its specific contribution, identifying the social, political, and eschatological dimensions of Jesus' utopic practice. Liberation must always be concrete, since oppression is concrete. The consecrated formulae of "integral liberation" must be interpreted correctly here. They must not be allowed to deprive Christian practice of its concretion, or to eviscerate the objectively theological content of the economic, political, and social liberations attained by the people. The point of the "integral" in the formula is to ensure that liberation will be an open process, embracing the entire being of the individual and society, and all its individuals and societies.

Culture is comprehensive. It embraces all the elements of personal and social existence. Evangelization, too, must therefore be comprehensive. How do cultures and subcultures assimilate the evangelical utopia? We must not limit the object of evangelization to the great cultural blocs: the poor, blacks, the Indians, mestizos, women, and so on. It is important to grasp the specificity of each subculture, which is constituted by the characteristics conferred on their practice by entire groups of society. Thus, there is a culture of work, a culture of communication, of scholarship, of the world of science, of the arts, of leisure, of children, of youth. Each of these realities, which make up the world of culture and society, calls for a specific evangelizing approach. The various social ministries of our local churches have concerned themselves with these matters extensively, both practically and theoretically. We must not lose sight of this effort when addressing the relationship between evangelization and cultures.

CHALLENGES FOR EVANGELIZATION TODAY

The following are significant points constituting a particular challenge for the gospel-culture relationship.

ON A WORLD SCALE

I have already cited the great current, global challenge: the future of life. Evangelization today must make an option for life against the mechanisms of death. "Life" is to be taken in its most rudimentary sense here, as continuation and subsistence of a life system threatened with collective collapse. Here the basic question is not how and to what extent cultures assimilate the gospel, but to what extent the gospel preserves the cultures from utter destruction. Paraphrasing Las Casas, we might say: better a live pagan culture than a dead evangelized one. To take up the cause of life, the means of life, to help develop a full ecological sense of love, respect, and preservation of every kind of life (everything alive deserves to live) is itself to effect the core of the gospel of the one who said: "I have come to bring life, and bring it in abundance" (John 10:10). This quest for life is undertaken in obedience to the gospel, and not merely in function of a survival instinct. Christianity, on the strength of its internal motives, must make its contribution to a response to this universal challenge of the preservation of the sacred system of life.

IN LATIN AMERICA

Puebla has bequeathed us a fundamental criterion of evangelization, applicable in all its precision to Latin America:

> The Church has been acquiring an increasingly clear and deep realization that evangelization is its fundamental mission; and that it cannot possibly carry out this mission without an ongoing effort to know the real situation and to adapt the gospel message to today's human beings in a dynamic, attractive, and convincing way. [Puebla Final Document, no. 85]

Evangelization emerges from the encounter between the Christian message and the challenges of reality. Without this dialogue, evangelization is either the imposition of a message, or a religious alienation without roots in culture.

Where the evangelization of the conflict-ridden reality of Latin America is concerned (as Puebla has analyzed that reality [Puebla Final Document, nos. 15–71]), we must consider the phenomenon of the historical dependency of this continent, which is at the origin both of its oppression, and of its counterpart, the yearning for autonomy and the liberation process. Christianity can become a wellspring of liberation, just as it was by and large a bulwark of the established order during the colonial period. Furthermore, this continent is characterized by huge social fringes of poverty and marginalization, among blacks, Indians, women, and workers. An evangelization that does not denounce the historical injustice of this situation and, from its proper standpoint of faith, become a potential for popular mobilization, liberation of the oppressed, and celebration of struggle, will find it difficult to be exonerated from the allegation of complicity with the order of domination and infidelity to Jesus' utopic dream.

Especially to the blacks, our churches owe a debt of justice. Institutionally, the churches were a good deal closer to the manor house than to the slave quarters. They must recognize the originality of black culture and the legitimacy of black religions, and welcome the process of syncretism that this culture and these religions have built as a form of resistance and acculturation of Christianity within the straitened confines of slavery. The case is the same with the witness cultures of the Amerindians. The church in Latin America must recognize the Indians' religions, the grandeur of their cultures, and their right today to a biological recovery, together with the reanimation of their cultural matrices and an assimilation of modernity and the Christian message after their own fashion.

We face the tremendous challenge of discovering pathways along which the Indians may have access to a Christian message emancipated from the cultural and institutional interests in which it has always been packaged. For certain segments of the Latin American church, new evangelization may mean a radical option: profound respect for the culture and religions of the Indians; support for the organizations working for their relative autonomy; backing of anything that may result in a demographic recovery on the part of the native races. What could be better news for the dominated but surviving cultures of the Incas, Mayas, Aztecs, Quechuas, Tupi-Guaranis, and others, than that they can rely on the support of sectors of the church to help recover their identity itself—including their religious identity?

The Latin American churches as a whole have historical ties with a type of institutional presence now five hundred years old. They feel a responsibility for the prolongation and improvement of this presence. With all the reforms and new initiatives that have been introduced, they still carry the stigma of the conquest of souls essential to the colonial project. This should not be a pretext for omitting evangelization in a framework of this reality. But it is possible that significant segments of the Latin American church might inaugurate a new, radical practice of solidarity: a journey with the Indians in their autonomous recovery, a reduction of explicit evangelization to a minimum, for now, in an awareness that the good news must come by way of this first mediation (the gospel of solidarity), as the indispensable basis of an explicit, truly liberative, evangelization. Native peoples must be rescued as a people, in order that, by faith, they may themselves become people of God. Five centuries of resistance must not have been in vain. The church is also responsible for seeing to it that this unspeakable suffering will have been conducive to the constitution of the people of God of Amerindia.

Economic Level: Labor. The economic level of evangelization must begin with a forthright and solid option for work over capital (in the vein of John Paul II's *Laborem Exercens*), inasmuch as the latter continues to hold the former under its domination. Here we face the phenomenon of the economically poor, who are the vast majority in Latin America. There is the risk of diluting the reality of the true poor, the economically poor, in the name of a broader concept of evangelical poverty, which includes other dimensions than the economic. Evangelical poverty is certainly a polyvalent concept, but its conceptual richness must not be bought at the price of forgetting of the scandalous material poverty that directly affects biological subsistence. Unless we attack this kind of poverty directly, in the name of Jesus and the apostles, as a challenge to evangelization, we shall be mocking the poor, by handing them an opiate religion, a religion that answers their cry for help with cynicism.

Not without reason did James, Peter, and John, the pillars of the primitive community, after approving the orthodoxy of Paul's gospel to the pagans, entrust him with caring for the poor, which he "sought to do with great solicitude" (Gal. 2:10), from the very outset of his mission. Evangelization in a context of impoverishment must join with other social forces as a factor for the generation of a society based on the toil of all, a society that prioritizes sharing over accumulation, and subjects the economic process to the control of society rather than to the demands of the market.

Political Level: Participation. Latin America has passed from the colonial regime to that of the "democraships"—the strong regimes dominated either by a national elite in collusion with the transnational corporations, or by the military, who have interfered and who still interfere in politics in the name of the interests of the possessors of capital. The churches have kept somewhat aloof from this process, endorsing, as a rule, the established order, which is antipopular, exclusive, and inegalitarian. Evangelization faces the challenge of encouraging Christian participants who seek the transformation of society, in order that, in a network of new social relations, there may be more justice, more group integration, and better living conditions for all. Such gains are not only political advances, they are boons of the reign, sought as such by evangelization. For us today, democracy, in a participatory, popular shape, is a historico-social means of achieving results understood by faith to pertain to the gospel project.

Symbolical Level: Utopias of Freedom. Economic and political domination is always accompanied by symbolical and cultural domination. The dominant symbolism on our continent is that of a foreign elite, which has fostered a historical contempt for popular culture, that of the blacks and Indians. The church in Latin America, which claims to be developing a new evangelization, will have to make an unequivocal option for popular culture, for the manifold expressions of the cultures of silence that today cry out for liberation. Popular culture is steeped in religion. It perpetuates memory of the people's failed struggles, and hope in the great utopias of liberty of which the dominated have never ceased to dream. A church will be popular to the extent that it permits the people to express themselves symbolically, in their own code, in ecclesial space.

Ecclesial Level: A Community Church. To this very day, we of the West know only the official version of Christianity, fragmented into various confessions partly as a protest against Roman centralization. On the outskirts of official Christianity, a popular Christianity has arisen, perpetually suspect of failing to maintain the whole of orthodoxy. But it is through this popular Christianity that the people, marginalized in society and the church, have expressed their faith and sustained their encounter with God. Today, gradually, a community Christianity is taking shape. This new expression has found its most consistent embodiment in the base Christian communities. Here faith is experienced as an impulse for the transformation of life. Here the gospel meets the reality of injustice, and kindles a yearning for liberation.

In this way, the new Latin American evangelization is conducting an experiment in ecclesiogenesis: the people themselves, poor and professing, are carrying forward the gospel project. Thus they become people of God. This pilgrimage will surely see the blossoming of a new profile of Christian — ecumenical, democratic, militant, struggling for a new society, and within that society, for a new church.

Personal Level: An Integral Evangelization. Evangelization projects a personal utopia as well — the utopia of the new man and new woman. After the example of Jesus of Nazareth, it seeks a new integration of the human person, centering on the values of freedom, creativity, and relationality. Each person is a knot of interrelationships, which stretch out in virtually every direction. Christianity sharpens the potential for communion, reference to others, and freedom. In Latin America the challenge is to live this quest for integral humanity in solidarity and communion with the struggle of the oppressed, who are denied the opportunity for personalization. Accordingly, personal liberation retains its evangelical status only to the extent that it manages to maintain an intimate nexus with social liberation. Wherever we are, wherever we live and breathe, we must put the utopia of the new, experienced as a leaven, into practice. This is a condition for projecting it on to the whole of society.

Pedagogical Level: The Process of Dialogue. Finally, pervading all these challenges, there is a pedagogical challenge. *How* are we to make evangelization liberative? This question is of fundamental importance, since, as the practice of Jesus and the apostles shows, method pertains to the very content of evangelization. The early missionaries had this concern, as well: they used theater, dramatization, and music, and immediately learned the native language, all in order to be able to transmit the gospel message.

There was, however, no attempt at dialogue with the cultures of the native inhabitants of this continent aimed at enabling them to appropriate the gospel (in an authentic syncretism).

Pedagogy was at the service of the content of the Christian message alone, and the content was laden with Western trappings: natives and blacks were obliged to undergo Roman Catholic circumcision. Hence evangelization's meager fruit, and the constant lament that the Indians were learning little or nothing. Today we understand that evangelical pedagogy must involve evangelized and evangelizer in the same process. Both must be evangelized, exchanging religious experiences, listening to each other, validating each other's differences, acknowledging the presence of the Word and the Spirit in each other, grasping their respective limitations and raising their consciousness of their joint mission to serve the world and the subworld of the oppressed: the gospel is for the redemption of humanity, and it begins with the victims of history.

The pedagogy developed in Latin America as a pedagogy of the oppressed, as a practice of freedom, and as the art of working with the people to develop their autonomy and capacity for free relations,[27] is especially valid when it comes to the process of evangelization, which must take its point of departure in oppressed cultures. An example of evangelization in a liberative pedagogical perspective is the account of the apparitions of Our Lady of Guadalupe to the Nahuatl (Aztec) Indian Juan Diego (examined in detail below). The churches have never learned this lesson. They have remained almost exclusively attached to the miraculous character of the apparition. But here, at the very dawn of evangelization, heaven itself supplied the most adequate method of synthesizing gospel and native culture. Our work today should consist in continuing this same approach. Only thus will evangelization be authentic, as well as liberative, and penetrate the cultural matrices.

Many are the challenges of a new Latin American evangelization. It must consist in a collaboration of the gospel with all the historical forces that one day will forge a new society. What God wills and loves is not first and foremost the church, but a new society. The new church will be found within that society.

PART 2 | Minimum Content for a New Evangelization

Part 1 of this book established the basic interrelationships that must prevail between faith and cultures in the Latin American framework. It was a kind of fundamental theology of mission, a missiological reflection, for today—for the level of theological awareness developed and for the degree of "conscientization" or consciousness raising that has been attained among Christians when it comes to social problems.

The next task will be to establish a minimum content for this new evangelization. Obviously I have no intention of sketching a "minimum catechetics"—the minimally complete content of a potential evangelization of cultures. My intent is a good deal more modest. The question is: How is the doctrine of God, Christ, and the Holy Spirit to be presented, and how is the church to be conceptualized, in this new evangelization? The approach will be dialectical: examining how, on the one hand, official dogmatic understanding helps to illuminate the problem of evangelization and cultures; on the other, how the challenges of this area, analytically identified, help us to shed light on and enrich our official dogmatic understanding.

Finally, I must not fail to deal with the problem of pedagogy, which pervades all the themes of evangelization. It will not be enough to solve the question of faith and cultures theologically. I absolutely must see how evangelization operates. I am not dealing with a purely technical problem: this is a question of content, since method itself belongs to the content of evangelization.

Before addressing this subject, let us attempt to grasp how the new evangelization relates to the first, classic evangelization of Latin America.

9 | From a Colonial Evangelization to a Liberative Evangelization

The first evangelization in Latin America took place under the sign of subjugation, and gave rise to a colonial Christianity, reproducing the religious models of the metropolis.[1] The new evangelization is taking place under the sign of liberation, and has shown itself capable of originating a typically Latin American Christianity of native, black, mestizo, white, and Latin stamp, innovative in terms of church structure. This Christianity does not suppress the first; it integrates it in the act of transcending it. In what does the difference between the first evangelization and the new one now underway consist?

The first evangelization occurred at the intersection of two forces: the expansion of Iberian commercial interests, and the reinforcement of the Christian image of the world as *orbis Christianus*. The colonization of Latin America, Brazil in particular, took place in order to enrich the mercantile establishment and the crowns of Spain and Portugal. What was produced in the New World was what was indispensable, complementary, and profitable for the central economies, and it was produced by way of forced labor, with an eye to greatly increased accumulation. An abundant work force was needed to implement this strategy. As Portugal and Spain could not furnish an adequate work force, natives were pressed into service. When these broke under the strain, blacks were brought over from Africa. The military and economic conquest of the Amerindian lands took place. Then the second conquest followed—the cultural and spiritual, by way of catechesis. The "other" (Indians and blacks) must become the "same" (Iberian Christians). In the dominant ideology of the time, the *orbis Christianus* represents the order willed by God on earth. Popes, kings, and princes must spread this order by every means at their command. Pope Alexander VI's bull, *Inter Caetera* (1493), is a fine example of this outlook—the understanding in which Latin American evangelization was steeped:

> Let the Catholic faith and the Christian religion, especially in our times, be exalted, and everywhere spread and propagated. Let the salvation of souls be procured. Let the barbarian nations submit, and let them be reduced to the faith.

Apart from this order, all else is perversity and disobedience. Thus, the Moors must be subjugated, as well as the Indians and blacks. The order willed by God constitutes a political and religious monolith. Evangelizing the natives meant introducing them to the *orbis Christianus*. That is, it meant making them Portuguese and Spanish. In terms of pastoral theology, evangelization was bound up with a Luso-Spanish cultural circumcision. Transplanted to villages and reductions, the Indians were turned into Portuguese or Spaniards, Christianized to the point that, in Anchieta's expression, there was "no longer anything Indian about the Indian."[2] The Indians were now someone else. This was symbolized by the loss of their own names, and their replacement with other names, given by the missionaries.[3] Completely uprooted from their culture, and deprived of that mainstay of every primitive culture, religion, the Indians—and then, in systematic, cruel fashion, the blacks—entered into the logic of the commercial project: they were used as a servile work force. Evangelization meant indoctrination in a codified, readymade faith. There was no intercultural dialogue to give rise to a possible new version of faith with native and black cultural instruments. Catechesis destroyed both, compelling them to conform to Iberian usages and customs. Once they had been acculturated, they were both subjected to forced labor. Evangelization, then, was colonial. The ideology of *orbis Christianus* — the only possible legitimate order in the eyes of God—bonded traders with missionaries. The missionary was inculturated, while the trader was enslaved.

THE THEOLOGY UNDERLYING COLONIAL EVANGELIZATION

What theology underlies this colonial model? Four points merit consideration:

1. *Identification of the reign of God with the church.* God's entire salvific design has been embodied in the church. Without its activity, nothing can occur that is eternally valid for human life. Hence the fervor of salvationist pastoral practice. It was urgent that the greatest possible number of persons be baptized, so as to afford them entry into heaven; otherwise they would be destined for hell. The death of baptized children was the occasion of joy. "It was these who, although of this earth, were destined for heaven, and before wickedness could change them, the Lord snatched them away."[4] It was difficult for the missionaries of the time to see any other expressions of the reign of God, such as in Indian or black worship, or in the everyday life of persons regardless of religious confession.

2. *Identification of the church with the Christian world.* Church and *orbis Christianus* were simply identical. Religious power and political power reinforced one another, as each strove for the construction of the same kind of society: one impregnated with the medieval religious view. To be a Christian meant to adopt Christianized culture. Faith and religion, gospel and world, were identified. Hence the understanding of the colonial process as a unified undertaking, commercial and missionary. Both were at the service of the order willed by God on earth, and both strove to build the reign of heaven in this history of ours.

3. *Identification of the Christian world with the world as such.* The only valid world is the Christian world. Accordingly, all other peoples must be incorporated into the Christian world. For the Indians, wrote Anchieta, "there is no better preaching than the sword and the iron rod."[5] There were those who saw a sign of God's providence in the thirst for the precious metals

that brought about the encounter with the Indians, and thereupon their conversion. These slaves should actually count themselves fortunate: by baptism they had begun to belong to the Christian world, and had thus escaped eternal damnation.[6] The ethical aberrations of the Portuguese and Spanish baptized were regarded as solely the perversions of individual Christians; they were never seen as an expression of a possible injustice on the part of the system itself. The Christian system, in the understanding of the time, was sound, and therefore untouchable.

4. *Identification of otherness — anything different — as the work of the devil.* Otherness was either a manifestation of paradise (the vision of paradise enjoyed great currency among the first navigators), and then it was accepted as innocent, or else it was held to be an expression of the anti-order, whose covert causal agent is the devil. A pitiless struggle raged between traditional healers and missionaries. Traditional practitioners were frequently labeled falsifiers of the truth and agents of the devil, and their knowledge was contemned as "diabolical."[7]

This process of identification resulted in Iberian society, and Christianity within it, presenting themselves as monoliths, complete unto themselves, intolerant and authoritarian, seeing themselves as the exclusive vehicles of salvation and of the criteria of what is good and evil and pleasing or displeasing to God. The social and ideological conditions of the time did not permit the recovery — without producing a crisis in the system — of the relevance of the traditional doctrine of God's universal revelation and of the seeds of the Word disseminated in human cultures. Such theological elements would have enabled the missionaries (as indeed occurred with a number of them, especially in Mexico) to strike an intercultural dialogue, and would have afforded them the openness necessary to create an Amerindian church (which indeed Bartolomé de Las Casas planned in his later years).[8] There was evangelization, but it was accompanied by subjugation. Colonial Christianity is profoundly contradictory, then. It maintains and fosters a liberating discourse, intrinsic to the good news. But that discourse is divorced from a liberating cultural and political practice. This is the tool of a colonial framework that only reproduces its social and religious institutions. Still, one fact must not be lost from view: colonial evangelization preserved a seed of freedom,[9] which one day could be extracted from its burial place. Then history could take its course.

THE THEOLOGY UNDERLYING LIBERATIVE EVANGELIZATION

It seems to me that that day has arrived for Latin America. The new evangelization has already been given conscious, official expression in the document "Evangelization in the Present and Future of Latin America," the Puebla document of 1979. The new evangelization incorporates everything that has occurred in five hundred years of proclaiming and living the Christian message, and now proceeds to a spiritual discernment: it now takes account of the limitations and distortions imposed on it by virtue of its ties to the colonial project.

This is where conversion comes in—a breach with a certain kind of past and with certain mental and institutional models of church. Finally the time has come to venture on the new evangelization under the sign of dialogue—of encounter between faith and subjugated cultures, and between cultures of witness and new cultures, in a perspective of integral liberation. The church must now present itself no longer as a closed, finished reality, to be implanted, but as an open reality, to be constructed, in contact with the contradictory reality that has taken shape on this continent. Puebla furnished the key to the pastoral theology of this process of a new evangelization, an evangelization that will bestow a new historical model on the church, in the celebrated no. 85 of its Final Document, where evangelization is asserted always to take place in intimate connection with historico-social reality.

In this encounter, reality is not only perceived, but is subjected to a critical analysis, and deciphered in its mechanisms of division between the rich few and the many poor. The hunger for God awakened by the colonial evangelization, joined to the hunger for bread that we see around us today, gives birth to an evangelization of liberation. The inculturation of the gospel must be effected, Puebla insists, in a "dynamic" way. That is, it must not be the mere repetition of what has already been said and taught; it must be something vital, flexible, something that will demonstrate the humanizing potential of the Christian proposition. It must occur in an "attractive" way. That is, it must be put into a form fitted to the mentality of our times, and to the way the unschooled, impoverished majorities learn. It must be presented in a "convincing" way. In other words, it must engender a new sense of life. And it will do so only if it exercises its charism of prophecy against the historical oppression suffered by the continent, and its charism of liberation in creating the new, the alternative, drawn from the deposit of faith.

In this evangelical process, evangelizer and evangelized are not two factions of the church. They evangelize each other, mutually, thereby building a church that will be a community of sisters and brothers, all of it ministerial, servant, and missionary. What is under way in Latin America, under the impulse of the Spirit, is an immense ecclesiogenesis—the genesis of a church, from the confrontation of the gospel with a world of injustice and poverty, in which the gospel demonstrates its liberative power. The following chapters outline the theological and ecclesiological criteria of this new, liberative evangelization.

10 | The Triune God Always Arrives before the Missionary

The first missionary and evangelizer is the divine Trinity itself. If we had a correct representation of God, always as a communion of the three divine Persons, inviting creation and all men and women to share in its communion, we should then easily understand the divine presence in history. Well did John Paul II say, to the Latin American bishops gathered at Puebla: "Our God, in his most intimate mystery, is not a solitude, but a family."[10] Thereby the pope sought to emphasize the character of *koinonia* that constitutes the essence of the trinitarian mystery.[11] The Christian God is an eternal, essential communion among the divine Three, a communion that overflows the inner life of God and bestows itself on the human persons of history, impelling them to seek and to live in communion among themselves, in family and society. We must see human societies, the social relationships among their members, their insatiable quest for sharing, communion, and a common life as impulses poured forth into history by the most holy Trinity, pale reflections of its own internal communion. Certainly there are divisions, class struggle, and sin, but these do not prevail over the dynamism that thrusts in the direction of sociability and a community of brothers and sisters.

The missionary is either a contemplative and mystic, or is no authentic missionary at all. The true evangelizer is imbued with faith in the concrete presence of the Trinity in every crease of the fabric of history, despite the splotches and blotches of human perversion. In the highly socialized forms of life of the Aztecs, in the uprisings of the Indians of Brazil, in the profoundly egalitarian sense prevailing among the majority of the native tribes of Brazil, the authentic missionary discerns sacraments of the trinitarian communion, and signs of the presence of Father, Son, and Holy Spirit in the world. The missionary always comes late: the Holy Trinity has already arrived, ever revealing itself in the awareness, the history, the societies, the deeds, and the destiny of peoples. This is why Vatican II taught, with reference to the missionary nature of the church: "It originates in the mission of the Son and the mission of the Holy Spirit according to the design of the Father" (*Ad Gentes*, no. 2). Hence its eminently trinitarian character.

In Latin America, the new evangelization must create, as Puebla so earnestly desired, communion and participation, and this from a point of departure in the forces of communion and sharing that the Trinity itself has aroused in the traditions and cultures of these lands.[12] It is not a matter of implanting imported models; it is a matter of "potentiating," multiplying exponentially, what the Trinity and women and men will build through the centuries. An evangelization that fails to make its contribution to the enormous gestation process of a society of solidarity, structured in participation, equality, diversity, and communion, has not accomplished its theological task, nor served the God-in-Trinity who seeks to be recognized and professed in human practices.

11 | The Eternal Word Incarnate and Raised Is Always Active in Cultures

Saint John says that "the Word enlightens every human being coming into this world" (John 1:9). And the eternal Word is the full revelation of the Father, within and without the trinitarian circle. All creation bears its stamp, since it is the archetype of all created being (cf. John 1:3, Col. 1:16, Eph. 1:22). This New Testament teaching is the origin of the patristic doctrine, in Saint Justin, Clement of Alexandria, and others, of the "seeds of the Word" that have been sown in all cultures.[13] All that is true, wise, intelligent, and productive of meaning and light, finds its ultimate origin in the eternal Son and Word itself. Recent documents of the magisterium have endorsed this teaching.[14] Modern evangelization needs all the value and validity of this tradition. Seeds that have not been recognized, or allowed to grow—of Maya, Aztec, Nahuatl, Inca, Tupi-Guarani, and other wisdom, the sacred books of the Central American sages[15]— must be recognized for their high value. All these religious contributions must be regarded as "arms that reach to heaven" (*Evangelii Nuntiandi*, no. 53), as responses called forth by the Word in the name of the Trinity. They have permanent value, inasmuch as they are the "living expression of the soul of vast human groups" (ibid.), and forms of encounter between human beings and God, and between God and the sons and daughters of God.

In the light of the fullness of revelation occurring in Jesus Christ, they can and must be seen as a kind of Old Testament. As they are indwelt by the eternal Word, they already contain the substance of the New Testament (in virtue of the oneness of revelation, testified to by Old and New Testament alike). We ought to allow Indians and blacks to fashion a biblical experience in their own manner, as, for example, Genesis is the fruit of dialogue and assimilation of many Middle Eastern creation myths on the part of Jewish monotheistic faith. The Jews did not reject what they found. They filtered all the data in the light of faith in the one God of creation. In much the same way, the Wisdom books of the Bible retain their Egyptian and Mesopotamian influence. The Indians and blacks who embrace Christ's promises must be permitted to shape their own syntheses of faith, using the elements of their cultures.

Roman Christianity is the result of the encounter of biblical faith with the Jewish culture of the diaspora, Hellenism, Roman culture, the contribution of the Germanic peoples, and modern thought. The rise of a Latin American Christianity—an Amerindian, black, mestizo, and white Christianity—can be fostered in the same way. This synthesis can emerge only from a boundless faith in the power of the gospel, with the courage to take on "witness cultures" and impregnate them with the Christian leaven. There will surely be purifications and rejections, but these cultural matrices embody divine revelation in their own ways. Without ceasing to be what they are, they will be tinged with an expression that assumes, uplifts, and fulfills what the Word itself had already built, in cooperation with men and women. Non-Christian religions are not realities external to Christianity. They are steeped in something that we find everywhere active: the Word that acts within them and within Christianity.

THREE DIMENSIONS OF INCARNATION

This eternal, universal Word became incarnate and particularized in the earthly reality of Jesus of Nazareth. Among the dimensions of the mystery of the incarnation are three that bear emphasis here.[16]

There is an undeniably ontological dimension, developed by the Council of Chalcedon (451): the divine nature, by way of the Person of the Word, is joined to a real, historical, biological, and cultural human nature. Thus the humanity of Jesus actually becomes the humanity of God. This consideration prescinds from the concrete, conflictive, and limited determinations within which the mystery is realized. It seeks to underscore the fact that it is possible for human nature to undergo this radical unification with the divinity "without confusion, without change, without division, and without separation" (the terms of the christological dogma of Chalcedon). From that moment forward, the destiny of human nature is definitively assured, since that destiny now belongs to the history of the eternal Son himself, and through this history to that of the whole Trinity. This major fact of our faith founds the so-called law of the incarnation. The Son assumes everything: nothing is excluded (except sin – Heb. 4:15 – which is a defiled moral relationship).

This divine logic inspires an analogous behavior in Christians. Confronted with the "other," they ought to assume that other integrally – permit a synthesis of the cultural given, and the Christian message to bloom from within. As the Son, in assuming human condition, conformed himself to it, so should it be, analogously, with mission and evangelization: one ought to be a Zapotec with the Zapotec, a Tukano with the Tukano, an Aymara with the Aymara. In the light of the mystery of the Incarnation, we can say: it is possible for culture to maintain its full identity, and still incorporate the Christian mystery, without separation and without confusion. In other words: each people ought to be able to be the people of God without having to pass through the mediation of the people who first recognized that it was loved by God, and thereby was constituted people of God, the Jewish and Christian people.

Secondly, the incarnation permits us to transcend the seeming incompatibility of transcendence and immanence. These two categories, of Greek extraction, have penetrated Christian reflection. They have introduced a serious danger of misunderstanding the Christian novelty: either that of spiritualization or that of secularization. Faith is articulated from a starting point in transcendence, and then immanence loses its weight and Christianity takes the shape of something ahistorical, something foreign to real processes, and irrelevant for the everyday. Or faith is articulated from a starting point in immanence, and then transcendence seems superfluous, and Christianity can be traded for secularism and become predominantly a religious power with a mighty influence on the political and the worldly. The incarnation teaches us to regard transcendence within immanence. The result is the transparency of immanence and the historization of transcendence. Their mutual transparency joins them together without destroying their particularity, just as the divine and human natures of Jesus are joined without any confusion or separation.

In terms of the matter under consideration here, this means: evangelization must render transparent a world touched by faith. The price of this transparency is the purification and refinement of every datum, without, however, losing or replacing that datum. The Indians must not lose their native sensitivity in embracing the Christian message. They must feel themselves even more radically native, and experience Christian faith as a "potentiation" of their native being. This challenge may seem utopian. But it is in the direction of this utopia that the path of the gospel must tend in the history of every people.

The third element present in the mystery of the incarnation, and of particular urgency for our subject, is how it was expressed in history and society. How, concretely, did Jesus of Nazareth experience his divine filiation, and under what material and cultural conditions did he organize his evangelizing practice? It is here that Christians will gain inspiration for the discharge of their task of authentic evangelization. Certain points need further emphasis.

JESUS AS EVANGELIZER: PARADIGM OF ALL EVANGELIZING PRACTICE

The gospel is always a reality charged with a vital, definitive meaning: the victory of the power of God over the evil powers of this world, and the full integration of creation into God's plan (the reign of God).[17] The gospel, to borrow the felicitous expression of Paul VI, is "the proclamation of a liberative salvation" (*Evangelii Nuntiandi*, no. 8). In the gospel, as we may gather from Jesus' practice, there is always an element of proclamation and great hope: "The reign of God is in your midst! The reign of God has come!" (Luke 17:21, Mark 1:15). To evangelize means to communicate a message that, in turn, contains a vision of the world, especially of its final destiny. But together with the message come signs. We behold deeds that transform reality, thereby evincing that the promises proclaimed are not imprisoned in desire and hope, but are already being fulfilled, and are creating a new history. Without the signs, the message would be pure theory. The signs alone, without the message to explain them, would leave evangelization in danger of becoming a system of assistance to human needs, which can never be completely satisfied. The signs are ordained to something greater: to a demonstration that the realization of the ultimate meaning here being concretely anticipated and shown is already taking its course in history. The concrete, meanwhile, is only a sign of greater things to come. In Jesus we always find a unification between proclamation and signs, message and practice.

IN HIS EVANGELIZATION, JESUS ALWAYS BEGINS WITH THE REALITY OF THE PEOPLE

First Jesus addresses their great hope of an overall, definitive solution to all their problems. He goes out to meet the people with the message of the reign of God, which represents the supreme utopia of his proclamation—a radical transformation of all relationships within creation—in such a way that God is seen really to be Lord, the giver of life and the full realization of the human being. Then he begins to attend to the most deeply felt and suffered existential ruptures: illness, discrimination based on religious preconceptions, the slavery of legalism, and the scapegoating of life at the hands of ritualistic religion.

Jesus' first public appearance, in the synagogue of Nazareth (Luke 4:16–19), demonstrates the unequivocal liberating tendency of Jesus' message. What is the great hope of the people today? The people hope for a just, participatory society, a new society. The people know, too, that this social reality will come only as part of something greater, which can only be a gift of God: new heavens and a new earth, human beings renewed at heart and reconciled with their origin and their end, God. An evangelization that fails to take up the radical hopes of the historical being of today, particularly the poor, would hardly be in continuity with and fidelity to what Jesus said and did.

Secondly, Jesus manifests enormous concern for existential ruptures—the conflicts that tear persons to shreds and rend the social fabric. Here we see the importance of Jesus' miracles of healing, of his attention to the poor and to public sinners, of his constant defense of the marginalized, the socially nonexistent. For Jesus, the world is not rosy, or exempt from conflicts. He does not maintain a serene, insensitive distance from the human drama, especially that of the powerless. He enters the conflict, and enters it on the side of those who suffer religious coercion and social domination. Jesus' option for the poor constitutes a part of his commitment to the Father and to the message of the reign. There is no pain that Jesus does not feel, no cry for help that Jesus ignores.

An evangelization that makes no effort to deliver the victims of the agonies of history (produced by structural, voluntary distortions), that fails to humanize existence, that fails to reduce the pain of life through the creation of a community of sisters and brothers (a messianic community), will have difficulty claiming to be in the tradition of Jesus. Unless Jesus is also the liberator *from* the human blemishes in which our sin is concretized, unless he is also liberator *for* higher forms of social relationship, personal and divine, he is not the Jesus of the gospel witness, but a fetish produced by and manageable by the interests of power and domination.

The gospels show that Jesus knew the life of the people—how planting is done, how to run a farm, how the unemployed behave in the market place, how bread is made, how weeds and wheat grow together, how festivals are celebrated, how families can suffer a falling-out, how to assuage the grief of a widow who has lost her only son, how the marginalized cry for help. He takes all this as material for his parables. He knows how to draw lessons from it all. He does not moralize: he takes reality as it is, with all its contradictions. He knows what there is in human beings—their attachment to comfort, their cowardice, but their courage and loyalty to the death, as well.

An evangelization that does not join faith to real life, that is unable to include in its discourse on God the manifold drama of existence, ends by alienating its hearers, and becoming historically irrelevant. It has almost nothing to say, because it does not take seriously what is serious and important for life.

JESUS' CONTEMPLATIVE VISION

Jesus is not someone who encounters God only in the classic loci of religion (prayer, scriptures, temple, synagogue, and so on). He possesses a contemplative view of reality. The Father steeps him in human experiences, and he lives in every situation. He contemplates how the lilies of the field grow, and how the birds of the air soar in freedom. He knows how seed behaves when cast on different kinds of soil. He knows the growth processes of the fig and the vine. But in these secular realities he discerns the presence of the reign, and the activity of divine providence. Rightly, then, can he say: "My Father is still working, and so I, too, work" (John 5:17). In other words: in all things, and not just in the law and the prophets, Jesus perceives the realization or the negation of the will of God.

An evangelization that failed to generate contemplation in the people, that failed to become a cultural element to the point where God enters into schemas of interpretation of reality, would not fully realize his mission. We must admit that the first evangelization, under the sign of subjugation, transmitted a piety that had its positive points, managing to introject into the mind of the people a strong notion of God as providence, the presence of God in suffering, the protection of the Blessed Virgin Mary, and the company of the saints. But this first evangelization failed to connect spirituality and politics, prayer and the ethical quest for justice.

THE POOR AS PRIMARY ADDRESSEES

Jesus never restricts the ambit of his message. It addresses all human destiny, eschatological as well as historical. However, he always begins concretely with the needy and poor.[18] His message is truly universal because it starts from them. If it were to leave them aside and address the religious or social elite, his message would be particularized. No one can remain indifferent to persons suffering; they are the repositories of universal causes: life for all, justice for all, rights for all.

Jesus' option for the poor means a protest against poverty, and an exaltation of the eminent worth and dignity of the person of the poor. Hence it is an expression of liberation from both poverty and wealth, and a call for the justice to be inaugurated by the messiah and his disciples. Only from a starting point among the poor is Jesus' message perceived as good news, since only in this way does it imply victory over the lassitude and helplessness to which the poor are abandoned. Jesus' messianic proposition brings with it an ideal of a society of brothers and sisters, a society of free, equal persons, as a sign of the reign already present in history.

An evangelization that does not directly involve the poor, and confirm their hope in a new, different society, an evangelization that does not take up the cause of the poor, their struggles and their lives, loses its Christian density, and betrays the historical Jesus, who was a poor person in this world, and who identified with the poor, appointing them his lieutenants at the crucial moment of history, in the hour of the definitive judgment upon the eternal destiny of persons and creation.

In Saint Matthew's perspective, the poor are not only the addressees of Jesus' good news, they are its content, as well.[19] The poor, as poor, whether or not they are good, are the object of the Father's love and Jesus' option. God as the God who gives life, and Jesus as the vehicle of life and of life in abundance (cf. John 10:10), bend over the poor, whose lack is precisely life, out of an exigency of the divine nature itself. It is in the poor that we perceive the nature of God: not a Being detached from our miseries, but a God who hears the cry of the oppressed, a God who acts in history, constructing the reign for men and women in freedom. No approach to evangelization may leave this perspective out of account, under pain of actually losing God and the lord Jesus who appeared in the form of a suffering servant among the poor.

RE-SOLUTION OF TRAUMATIC SITUATIONS

The good news of Jesus shows its goodness in its ability to generate meaning where existence seems to have failed. Whenever he is confronted with a traumatic situation, Jesus causes it to explode from the inside. He does not limit himself to mediocre solutions, prescribed by law or tradition. He surprises. He appeals to the most generous energies of the human being, as we see so clearly in the Sermon on the Mount. He does not simply wait for someone in need to live up to his expectations. He heals such a one, yes, but he solicits faith and discipleship. He forgives sins, but he also says: Go and sin no more!

The gospel cannot be divorced from its content: to Jesus, not everything is equally true. It has concrete statements about the Father, about the reign, about the importance of adhering to the one sent from the Father, about limitless love and mercy. But there is also an atmosphere of liberation, of ease, of benevolence, in contact with Jesus. So it brings an increase in feeling for life, in existential hope, in openness to the infinite, deriving from Jesus' practice and words.

Jesus comes forward as a great storyteller, whose meaning shines through the very terms of his narrative. A "disclosure situation" (Robinson), as the linguists say, is always created, a re-solution of dramas, a light that bursts forth and takes us by surprise, bestowing new heart on existence. By these mediations is manifested the salvation and redemption that God is effecting in the marrow of reality.

An evangelization that fails to "potentiate" life, multiply it exponentially, that does not relieve minds of their existential fears, that does not lead to social structures of greater collaboration and hence of humanization, will hardly bring Jesus' good news to the here and now.

METHOD, TOO, BELONGS TO EVANGELIZING CONTENT

There is more to the gospel than content and atmosphere. There is Jesus' pedagogy, too: the way in which he conveyed his proposition, and organized his practice. He establishes a dialogic structure. Never is he imposing, like a legalist or moralist who is ruled by the structure of authority. He makes the most of his hearers' existing knowledge. Never does he employ power as a mediation of the propagation of the reign and its message. He relies on persuasion, argumentation based on common sense, the deepest calls of one's being. The witness of his own life — that transparent witness of his — his devotion to others to the point of not having time to eat or sleep; his boldness in the denunciation of religious falsifications and the arrogance of those who wield religious power; the respectful, tender way in which he deals with those whom life has crippled and stigmatized—these are all elements of the gospel and suggestive data for his following. The way in which he confronts temptations, the conflicts with ideological opponents such as the Pharisees, the imminence of his violent death, become paradigmatic for Christians.

Evangelization in our day should be ruled by these methodological guidelines of Jesus. They are part of the mystery of the incarnation. Christians should renounce, once and for all, the use of political and cultural power to assert themselves and force themselves on others. These strategies do not show confidence in the interior strength of the gospel. They make it appear that it is not true in itself, but only "true" by dint of external imposition on the part of those who have the power to frame and subject bodies and minds.

There are subtle ways today of perpetuating the strategy of power as a tool in the propagation of the gospel: new movements of the dominant classes, new social subjects, transnationalized, reproducers of the system of domination and marginalization of the great majorities. They are generally progressive when it comes to the assimilation of modern techniques of effectiveness, but conservative in terms of the political aims. When it comes to facing serious social questions their trust is still in the old alliance of the church institution with the decision-making power centers of our laissez-faire bourgeois societies. They may do a great deal *for* the people and *for* the poor, but they never do it *with* the people and together *with* the poor, from the viewpoint of the poor. They end by eternalizing relations of dependency, and preventing the impoverished from becoming the subjects, the agents, of their own history.

THE CONFLICT INHERENT IN ANY EVANGELIZATION PROCESS

Evangelization as practiced by Jesus of Nazareth is always seen to comport an element of conflict.[20] This is inherent in the proclamation of the good news and the practice of the reign of God. Just as evangelization comports acceptance of the "other" (the affirmative element), as we have seen, it also comports the redemption of that other (the critical element). Acceptance does not legitimate what it accepts. It confronts this with the demands of the reign, the divine utopia. The church, like any other religious structure, discovers its insufficiency. All are called to transcend the given, the already accomplished, in the direction of what is yet to be done, and what must be transformed. This is how conversion applies as an ongoing reality, for Christians and non-Christians alike. Conversion does not mean conversion to the church, or to any particular expression of the gospel. It does not mean this primarily. Were this to be the case, the encounter would necessarily imply stripping the others of themselves and their cultural incorporation into the prevailing European-type Christianity.[21] Such a procedure would imply subjection, and not conversion, and it is a procedure that has been broadly implemented in Latin America.

This means that conversion is an ongoing process. In other words, conversion is a process from which the church may never exempt itself on the pretext of having already accepted the Lord and having expressed this process by baptism and incorporation into his community. The church must always be converted to its Lord, to the messianic utopia. And to be converted to others, as the Son of God was converted to others, as he turned to others, means to turn to the world, and to enter into it. And we observe that, in history, everyone has a special resistance to all self-transcendence, to denying oneself dialectically in order to be able to incorporate new elements and to keep oneself open to God and to the permanent novelty of history as the irruption of the Spirit itself. We know the tragedy of the element of ancient Palestinian culture that resisted the messiah and shut itself up in its own version of hope. We recognize that Roman Catholicism resisted the call of the great cultures, especially in the Orient, and to this day has not learned to penetrate them in creative fashion.

This conflictivity, then, is structural, and belongs to any authentic process of evangelization, embracing evangelizer and evangelized alike. The correct missionary strategy would be the following. The missionary is converted to the native or to the black, and these are converted to Christ. Once conversion to Christ has taken place, the missionary task has attained its goal. The result, then, is a native, Tupi-Guarani, Aztec, black, ecclesial community or church, which is also an expression of the *Catholic* Church—one of so many possible faces of the church of Christ and of the Spirit in history. Unless, in our own day, this process of conversion to the gospel, to others, to Christ, and to new forms of realization of the Christian mystery, is permanently maintained, there will be no authentic evangelization, which must be more than the simple expansion of the church system, and which must avoid imposing a new circumcision of Western, romanized imprint.

12 | The Holy Spirit: The Divine Imagination in Cultures

Christomonism (concentration of the entire Christian mystery in Christ) is partly responsible for missionaries' inability to see in other religions ordinary pathways of cultures in the direction of God. To Christ must always be joined a reading in terms of the Spirit. Well did *Ad Gentes* say: "Both [the Lord Jesus and the Holy Spirit] are always and everywhere joined in the realization of redemption" (no. 4). The Spirit, like the eternal, preexistent Word, is ever-present in history, impelling the dynamisms of life and growth. It is the Spirit who opens the church to new mission frontiers. Let me examine certain elements of pneumatology—necessarily omitting others, for lack of space—that can direct us in a quest for a new, liberating evangelization.[22]

THE SPIRIT IS THE PRINCIPLE OF LIVING TRANSCENDENCE

All cultures maintain an explicit or implicit reference to transcendence. History does not resolve itself, nor does the human mystery find within itself its convincing reasons for living. There is an appeal to the infinite, the persistence of the ultimate interrogation that the religions thematize. The Spirit is revealed in this imperishable dimension of human beings: their oceanic depth, their infinite desire for communion and eternal life. That the religions have endured to this day is testimony to the presence of the Spirit in the various cultures.

THE SPIRIT BREAKS INTO INSTITUTIONS AND INTRODUCES NOVELTY

Any institution, including the ecclesial and ecclesiastical institution, has a tendency to adapt to, and organize itself in terms of, institutional power. When an organism allows its organization to predominate, it runs a greater risk of becoming rigid and petrified. The Spirit appears in the emergence of the new, by forcing a breach in the institution. Then is when we see the surprise element, which begets a new hope and confers a new meaning on institutions.

In a pneumatological light, the church cannot contemplate itself as a finished reality, something constructed once and for all. As long as there are cultures that have not had their encounter with the gospel, that have not had their Christian experience (segments of a culture or the whole culture), the evangelizing mission cannot be said to have been accomplished. Resistance to the Spirit where new cultural expressions of the Christian message are concerned may constitute the major historical sin of Roman Catholicism. In important segments of its membership, it tends to regard itself as the full realization of the will of Christ, and the fulfillment of the messianic promises. Besides triumphalistic arrogance, this kind of attitude engenders an incapacity to perceive the potential of incarnation, and the way it can take virtualities of shape in the manifold cultures of the world. This kind of Catholicism appears to the eyes of others as a product of the West. In terms of world history it is increasingly seen as a regional phenomenon.

THE SPIRIT IS THE PRINCIPLE OF THE TRANSLATION OF JESUS' MESSAGE INTO TERMS SUITED TO THE PRESENT

Vatican II boldly formulated the law of all evangelization: "to adapt the gospel to the grasp of all as well as to the needs of the learned, insofar as such was appropriate" (*Gaudium et Spes,* no. 44). Theologically, the Spirit constitutes the force of invention of new meanings, and of different methods of reconciling human culture and the Christian message. The mission of the Spirit complements that of Jesus: "He will take of what is mine and will give it to you to know" (John 16:14); "he will bring to memory all that I have told you" (John 14:26), and will lead the disciples to the fullness of the truth (John 16:13–15). The full truth of Jesus is manifested in its various translations into different cultural expressions. It is the Spirit who refuses to allow the gospel message to remain *in illo tempore,* "at that time," in olden days, and leads it to develop its potential for new human and divine meaning in our times.

To reduce the gospel to a single valid expression is to condemn ourselves to mediocrity: it means we are attempting to compress mystery to the point where it can be forced into the dimensions of our head. It means refusing to accept the deeds wrought by God among the peoples, and preventing those deeds from coming to fuller expression in contact with the Christian mystery. At Pentecost the Spirit did not have everyone speak the same language — but rather brought it about that all, in their own languages, heard the same message of salvation (cf. Acts 2:11). In Latin America, Christ has not yet been adequately heard in the hundreds of languages of our various native cultures. It is not enough that he be heard in a variety of tongues: his actual meaning must also be expressed in the most diverse discourses and theologies.

THE SPIRIT AS PRINCIPLE OF LIBERATION OF THE OPPRESSED

Jesus' activity always stimulated the fullness of his addressees' freedom. "Where the Spirit of the Lord is, there is freedom" (1 Cor. 3:17). This freedom is a gift of the Spirit to those who struggle against oppression of every kind. Thus the Spirit is seen as *Pater pauperum,* "father of the poor" and oppressed who suffer in captivity and who long for liberty. It is the Spirit who bestows strength for resistance and survival, a courage for liberation that rattles prison bars, that stirs in the impoverished the creativity to open up new paths. The Spirit "directs the course of history . . . renews the face of the earth, is present to human development" (Paul VI, *Octogesima Adveniens,* no. 37). Saint Paul saw in the Spirit a power that delivered human beings from the regime of circumcision, establishing them in a position of direct access to Christ (cf. Gal. 4:6–7, 5:22–25).

Today, must we not see the activity of the Spirit in all of those evangelizers who attempt to recover the newness of the gospel and deliver it from the captivity of a misunderstood *Romanitas* that functions as a prohibition after the fashion of the old circumcision? The new evangelization will measure its truthfulness by the capacity it demonstrates to deliver the oppressed effectively, and to occasion the appearance of an Amerindian or Afro-Latin American church that will permit a more profound humanization of those who live their faith on this continent.

The Spirit is the divine imagination. It will not be hemmed in. It is the mobility of the church, its ongoing disinstallation, its dissatisfaction with itself, stimulating it to ever new efforts along the pathways of all peoples.[23]

13 | Toward a Church with Mestizo Features

Before we consider the model of church that must emerge from the new Latin American evangelization, we would do well to recall what Paul VI says in *Evangelii Nuntiandi* (1975): "The Church always has need of being evangelized." And "it begins [its evangelization of others] by evangelizing itself" (no. 15). I have already addressed this imperative in the first part of this book. It is of fundamental importance, as it is not customary for the institution to utter this kind of discourse or to take it seriously. But historical mistakes in this area have been so many, especially in the first evangelization of Latin America, that good sense simply requires it. We have seen that the church must be evangelized by Christians themselves, by exercising their office of prophecy in ecclesial space, and taking up the creativity permitted them by the gospel, rendering the community more participatory and egalitarian. The church must allow itself to be evangelized by current society (*Gaudium et Spes*, no. 44), something already examined in some detail. It must relearn the gospel from a point of departure in the poor (Puebla Final Document, no. 1147). Finally, it must be evangelized by those whom it claims to evangelize: in our case, by the blacks, the Indians, women, and the cultures of our continent. After all, all of these, by the deed and grace of mystery, are also mediators of the gospel of God.

EVANGELIZING BY CREATING FAITH COMMUNITIES

The first evangelization had a profoundly salvationistic concern. Evangelization was a matter of saving souls, which could not be saved outside the church. Of course Christians are concerned with the salvation of all. But we understand that this salvation is a permanent gift offered by God to all persons, through a thousand historico-cultural mediations. Salvation is a gift offered to all. This is guaranteed. The function of the church consists in sacramentalizing salvation in history—becoming a conscious sign and instrument of its implementation, especially among the poor and outcast. Concretely, the purpose of evangelization is to propose the Christian message, and to summon individuals and groups to personal adherence, and to express their faith in community. Then church becomes reality.

The most correct definition of church is that which understands it as a *faith community*—that is, a community born of faith in God who has sent the divine Son to fulfill us humanly and redeem us from our perversions in the strength of the Spirit of life and freedom. Evangelization is aimed not at individuals, but at persons in their social and community relationships. Unless evangelization produces the intrinsic objective of community, evangelization itself is not attained. When we speak of a faith community, we do not refer specifically to any particular type of social formation, but to various ways of living together. We refer to a spirit that should be present in all communities, regardless of their particular cultural shape, a spirit characterized by an immediacy of relationships and by a sharing of the same life, the same problems, the same solutions.[24] The new evangelization will be new only if it creates a Christianity of communities, and not a society of Christendom, massive, with its relationships anonymous, asymmetrical, and marked by a rigid division of function in the church (clergy on one side and laity on the other).

A COMMUNITY THAT CELEBRATES ITS FAITH AND LIFE

There is no faith community that does not celebrate its faith and the life illuminated by that faith. This is an essential part of church. This celebration should be marked by the memorial of the original, originating deeds that communicate the presence of Christ and his Spirit. But it will express these deeds in symbols—material elements and rites—drawn from surrounding culture. Here we must be consistent, and give full rein to the freedom and creativity permitted by a sound sacramental and liturgical theology, which has not misunderstood the principle *salva substantia sacramenti*. Correctly understood, the *substantia* of a sacrament is not primarily the materiality of the signs concerned, but the meaning conferred on these signs by Christ, who expressed that meaning in signs drawn from his Jewish culture. For example, in order to signify that he is life, he took as a cultural sign the bread that is the principal food of the Mediterranean culture. Had he wished to do this in Central American culture, he would have taken maize, or manioc, since that is what expresses life there. Among non-European cultures, then, the new evangelization must have the courage to choose the symbols of those cultures that express the divine mysteries. Otherwise those peoples will always be prisoners of a colonial conception of evangelization.[25]

A COMMUNITY OF LIFE, SERVICES, AND MINISTRIES

At the root of the community and its celebration is a communion of life and services. It is *koinonia*, communion, that guarantees the community's ecclesiality. All communion—we need not go into detail here—involves an exchange of experiences, the placing at the common disposal of all that affects the community, the common quest of the common good. There can be real communion only when the members of a community regard one another as equals, as brothers and sisters. Not all do everything. Each person has a function in the community. But this function is equally accepted and respected, without discrimination or marginalization. The various ministries and services in the community will be flexible, then, related to the demands of the community, and to the particular cultural formations of each people. Of course, there will be ministries that will permanently attend to the structural needs of the community, and of faith itself, such as proclamation, the administration of the sacraments, and the need for organs of coordination and support. But there will be other expressions as well, according to the typical idiosyncracies of each people.

An evangelization that accepts others and gives them room, so that various forms of church organization may appear, can be regarded as a new evangelization, one not merely reproductive of the institutional forms it has encountered in a Catholicism on the European model. Far from representing a threat to unity, these differences reveal the wealth of unity. And here it must be said that only those institutions arising out of the spirit of the people themselves, those formulations that translate a cultural mentality and do not represent the mere repetition of the memorized, received from on high and from without, can be authentically called evangelizing.

A COMMUNITY SERVICING INTEGRAL LIBERATION

Finally, any church community must exist for *service to others*. This is its mission. The church's mission derives its meaning from the mission of Christ: to bring life, and life overflowing (John 10:10). If the encounter with the gospel does not produce an exponential increase in meaning, an expansion of the dynamics of life, and a deepening of social relationships, up to and including the supreme expression of relationship, that with God, nothing will have been achieved. An authentic encounter with the gospel will introduce an element of destructurization into what the Word and the Spirit had previously wrought in history. We must say that, in a certain sense, and in not a few parts of Latin America, the arrival of missionaries meant the arrival not of the good news, but of bad news—the bad news of disease, exploitation, subjugation, and death. The God of life could be seen and rejected as the deity of death, as that God is indeed occasionally denounced by native healers and sages.[26] With the blacks and Indians, the church has lost a great part of its evangelizing credibility by reason of the political and social circumstances in which evangelization has taken place. There is little doubt that such an evangelization is destined to fail, and to produce an antigospel, when it is not carried out in a mystical vision, and in respect for the first evangelization, wrought by the Spirit and the Word in the hearts of persons and cultures. That this process is possible, that it engenders life, and a genuine evangelization from a starting point among the evangelized themselves, who in their own turn evangelize those who have evangelized them, can be seen in the case of the Little Sisters of Jesus (of Charles de Foucauld) among the Tapirapé natives.

In Latin America, evangelization will be new, and will not prolong the colonial project of subjection, only if it begins with the poor, and steeps itself in their lives, causes, and struggles. It is from among the poor, who constitute the majority of our populations, that the gospel shows its liberative force. If it is not liberative here, it will not be the gospel of Jesus, nor will its project of penetrating the cultures of others be legitimate. The heart of the Puebla document is the option of the church for the poor. With this option, Puebla swung wide the doors of human service to the life of those who are in need of life here and now, and who long for eternal life as well.

With what methods and strategies will this evangelization be carried out? I think there is a good answer in the form and content of the apparitions of our Lady of Guadalupe, which occurred at the dawn of the penetration of the gospel into this continent. Here was an authentic evangelization, paradigmatic in nature, and its lessons have not yet been sufficiently learned by our local churches. Let us examine this process.[27]

PART 3 | The Liberative Method of Our Lady of Guadalupe: The Amerindian Gospel

The question of method is never absent from the gospel. Jesus' own method, in a context of mission, makes an original methodological proposal: a complete self-stripping and a proclamation of peace (cf. Mark 6:7–11). And the whole history of the church is marked with the most heated debates over how to combine the obligation to preach the gospel with the necessary respect for human freedom. More and more, the Christian message is a proposal, not an imposition.

In the sixteenth century, because of the Conquistas, *that question returned with a vengeance, to remain with us ever since.*[1] *At bottom, it is in the solution of this problem that the question of the much heralded new evangelization will be solved. Is it really methodologically new, or,* fine finaliter, *will it repeat the mistakes of the past, and bring in little or nothing that is new? Throughout our considerations in this book, the matter has come up again and again. Let us deal with it explicitly, then, however succinctly, in the terms in which it was posited in the first beginnings of the* Conquista. *It is a problem that refuses to go away.*

14 | The Impasse of the First Evangelization: Absence of Dialogue with Native Religions

The "discoveries" (in the European perspective) and invasions (from the viewpoint of the natives) placed Christians before a series of problems that struck them as very complex.

The first was: Of what "nature" are the Indians? Are they human like ourselves, so that we must respect them, or are they beasts, which we may therefore subjugate? Not a few, especially among the *encomenderos* and colonists, must have regarded the Indians as animals, since that is how they treated them. The missionaries loved them with an absolute passion. But they loved them the way parents love their young children: they hated to see them grow up. They regarded the natives as children, without the full use of reason. They even denied they had the use of reason, claiming that only whites and mestizos had that.[2] In fact, this was one of several considerations that led the missionaries to bar natives from the priesthood, with disastrous consequences down to our own day.

The second question was: What right do Iberians have to seize Indian lands and wealth, destroy their temples, subjugate them, and make them Christians and subjects of the Spanish and Portuguese monarchs? This debate was the occasion of the appearance of the *jus gentium*, written by Francisco Vitoria and other great jurists and theologians of Salamanca and Valladolid.

The Iberian monarchs were most solicitous for justice and legality. And so they scheduled debates among the scholars of the time, in order to provide Iberian expansion with a theological and juridical foundation. In the colonies themselves, the argument was more pragmatic. No colonist had traversed the

Atlantic to till the soil. All had come that they might be the wealthy lords of glebe and vassal. They said: "It is better for the Indians themselves to be human slaves than free animals."

The third question was: How should the Indians be converted? Innumerable texts from the sixteenth century address this question, and the result is dramatic. On the Portuguese side we have the celebrated *Dialogue of Padre Nóbrega on the Conversion of the Heathen*.[3] From the Spaniards we have the famous text of Father José de Acosta, *De Procuranda Indorum Salute: Preaching the Gospel in the Indies*.[4] Acosta says that, after long meditation, he has arrived at the following conclusion: there are three methods of evangelization, as follows.[5]

The first method of evangelization is *apostolic*. One goes to the heathen without weapons, without any paraphernalia of power, armed only with the power of God's word. But this, Acosta points out, places the missionaries' lives at risk, since they are now at the mercy of the violence of the natives. Thus he does not recommend this first method.

The second method is *colonial*. First the natives are subjected to Christian sovereigns, then the gospel is preached to them. But this method places the lives of the natives at risk, as they are now at the mercy of the weapons of the colonists. This method is also to be rejected, then.

Acosta calls the third method the *"new way* of preaching the gospel, adapted to the new condition of these nations."[6] In what does the novelty of this condition consist? In its basis on the notion that the natives are "a mixture of man and beast."[7] But the method should match the situation. Therefore, the missionary approach should be to be humane in response to the natives' human side, and fierce in response to their savage or bestial side. How, then, is the gospel to be proclaimed in these conditions? In a "new way," mingling the good elements of both methods. The missionary is armed with the word of the gospel alone (from the apostolic method), but "moves about with human aids, and a patrol of soldiers to protect his life" (from the colonial method).[8] This is the preferred way. This, for Acosta, is the new evangelization for Latin America.

Indeed, this was the method that prevailed. Both Nóbrega and Acosta write its apologia. It produces immediate fruit. Fear subjects the natives politically (they acknowledge the Iberian monarchs, pay tribute, and accept the pope), and they enter the church, accepting the Christian message brought by the missionary.

This strategy created Latin American Christianity, an expansion of European Christianity. Christianity on the new continent was no novelty vis-à-vis European Roman Catholicism. It was a mere duplication of the latter. The novelty was to be in another enterprise, launched far from official control, in Latin American popular Catholicism, which was comprised of medieval elements — devotions to patron saints, vows, pilgrimages, shrines, confraternities, leagues — and elements assimilated from native and Afro-American religions.

Attempts at a peaceful evangelization, as we shall presently see with Las Casas, were the exception rather than the rule. There was a component of violence in evangelization.

As some Spaniards argued: "The voice of the gospel is heard only where the Indians also hear the cannon's roar."[9]

We must not lose sight of the matchless efforts of the missionaries to carry the Christian message to all the natives they found. A missionary mystique infected the entire Iberian Peninsula. The flower of the clergy and religious set out for the new world. Thousands perished before they even reached their missionary destinations, struck down by disease, wandering off-course and lost, or shipwrecked and drowned.

The missionaries used every imaginable method to draw the natives to the *orbis Christianus*.[10] First they learned their languages and dialects. They penetrated their cultures. Some, like the Franciscan Bernardino Sahagún, in Mexico, did actual historical and ethnological research on the myths and customs of Mexican Nahuatl culture. They opened schools where they could, like the famous one at Santa Cruz in Tlaltelolco for the sons of the Aztec elite. Within a few years the students of this school were using Spanish and Latin as in European Renaissance centers of learning.

Next they made catechisms, in pictures or words, in which Christian doctrine was presented in the form of stories that would be easy for the natives to understand. At other times they used music, as did Anchieta, the Franciscans and Jesuits in their reductions of California or Paraguay, and Bartolomé de Las Casas in his experiment with peaceful evangelization in Guatemala (Vera Paz). Not rarely, the missioners used theater and other kinds of dramatization. They went even further: from Hispaniola (Santo Domingo) they hoped to be able to select gifted young natives, dispatch them to Spain, where they would learn the Christian culture and religion, and then bring them back to share all of this with their Indian brothers and sisters. There was a remarkable case in Brazil: the Jesuits created a special catechetics for young children, rearing them in a boarding school and then returning them to their tribe to be the teachers of their parents and the other natives. Or there were the famous village settlements and reductions where, inspired by the utopia of Joachim of Flora and the utopic spirit of both the first Christians and the Renaissance, missionaries began to build a new humanity in a communist republic.

But what predominated was evangelization tied to colonialism. The cultural and religious process was an integrated one, imbued with a great deal of objective violence. The confrontation between Europeans and natives took place on a footing of profound inequality. There was no actual dialogue, in the form of mutual listening and reciprocal learning. What there was was direct domination, without euphemisms, of the natives by the invaders. And the colonists who came were adventurers, the refuse of Iberian society, some of them criminals, others in penal servitude, all of them obsessed by the myth of easy riches. They created the most scandal, undoing by bad example what the missionaries taught the natives with their catechesis.

Added to all this was the profound upheaval of native culture inflicted by the invaders. The missioners were always complaining that the natives retained next to nothing when it came to religious education. The problem was that the natives did not know—nor were they given any means of knowing—where to fit all this doctrinal content into the meaning framework of their cultures. Christianity had come like a bolt from the blue, and had left them totally confused and disoriented. It is easy to see why so many missionaries sought to separate the natives from the colonists in order to evangelize them, not only in order to conceal the scandals the colonists committed, but also, and especially, in order to be able to work directly with the population in a homogeneous and consistent way, "according to the political customs of Portugal and Spain." This was Las Casas's intent in founding a mission in Tierra Firme on the coast of Venezuela, an enterprise that eventually failed, as well as of the frequent petitions addressed by the Portuguese missionaries to the court in Lisbon.[11]

The royal doctrine and instructions were clear: evangelization must be peaceful and loving (as Columbus, too, was commanded by Ferdinand and Isabella on the occasion of his second voyage). But what was to be done if the natives resisted, and simply did not accept the gospel or acknowledge the sovereignty of the Spanish and Portuguese monarchs, or the pope as God's representative?

This question produced an immense "just war" literature, for the justification of aggression against the natives, in case they would show themselves too bellicose or refuse to welcome the gospel. Gonzalo Fernández de Oviedo (in his famous *General and Natural History of the Indies, the Islands and Mainland of the Oceanic Sea*), asked: "How can it be wrong? Gunpowder against the infidel, and incense for the Lord!"[12]

As we know, massacres of the natives were frequent. When Christopher Columbus landed for the second time, the missionaries ordained chastisement by fire and sword for the destroyers of the little fort left by the admiral on the occasion of his first voyage. Violence and disease had completely wiped out the native inhabitants of Santo Domingo before the end of the sixteenth century. As two colonists of that time put it:

> "It seems that it has pleased God Our Lord to do away with these Indian heathen altogether, whether because of the sins of their forebears, or of their own, or for some other, unknown reason; that these holdings may pass to your Majesty and his successors, and be populated by Christian folk."[13]

Despite the death to which fate had condemned the natives, the crown did manifest moral scruples. It was aware that the presence of the colonists meant a profound upheaval in the life of the native populations. A fruit of this questioning was the celebrated *Requerimiento*.[14] This was a theological and juridical document that was to be read to the natives officially (ideally in the presence of a notary) on their first contact with the Spaniards, justifying their subjugation and legally establishing the right of the Spaniards to evangelize them.

THE *REQUERIMIENTO*: INSTRUMENT OF NATIVE DOMINATION

Composed in 1514 by Juan López de Palacios Rubio, the *Requerimiento* opens with a historical account of the creation of the world. It then sets forth the establishment of the papacy as an instrument of divine representation, and concludes with the granting by Alexander VI to the monarchs of Spain of "these islands and mainland." The document requires (hence its name, *Requerimiento*) of the natives a twofold assent. First, they must acknowledge the "Church as sovereign mistress of the entire world, [with] its Supreme Pontiff, called the Pope, who has been pleased to establish the King and Queen as Lord and Lady and Royal Monarchs of these islands and mainland, in his name [and] in virtue of the said grant." Second, they must allow themselves to be instructed in the tenets of the true religion. Otherwise they would be subjected to the crown and the church by fire and sword.

The *Requerimiento* was expressed in the harshest terms:

> We shall take you, your wives, and your children, and shall make you slaves, sold or divided as shall please Their Highnesses; we shall take your goods, causing all the harm and destruction that we can, as to rebellious vassals who refuse to welcome their lord, who resist him and reject him; and we reassert that you, and not Their Highnesses, nor we, nor the knights who accompany us, will be responsible for the death and destruction that will befall you. And we require the Notary here present to attest in writing to all that we have told you, and to the reading of the *Requerimiento*, as we require that all others here present be able to testify as well.

With Las Casas, we "know not whether to laugh or weep" at this tragicomic display of arrogance. Our sense of the ridiculous is heightened when we learn that if the document could not be read in the presence of the natives, it was to be called out after them as they fled, or read to the crops or empty huts. The formalities must be observed, and the bad conscience of those who had subjugated the natives palliated.

THE PAPAL BULL: INSTRUMENT OF NATIVE LIBERATION

The colonists were so convinced that the natives were animals, or near animals, that Dominican missioner Bernardino de Minava had to make a trip to Rome to wrest from Pope Paul III, in 1537, the bull *Sublimis Deus*. It asserted that the Indians were endowed with reason, and that their lives and property were therefore to be respected.

Since it is the first papal document addressed to Latin America, we transcribe it here, in the form in which it is cited by Las Casas in the famous work of his upon which we shall presently be commenting, the *De Unico Vocationis Modo*.[15]

Paul, Bishop, Servant of the Servants of God. To all Christians who shall see these presents: Health and apostolic benediction.

The Most High God has so loved the human race that He created human beings in a condition in which not only could they share in what is good, like other creatures, but could actually attain to the Supreme Good itself, inaccessible and invisible though It is, and contemplate It face to face.

And as human beings were created that they might enter into life and the eternal blessings, as Sacred Scripture likewise attests; and as none can attain this everlasting life and bliss except by faith in Our Lord Jesus Christ; it must be confessed that human beings are of such condition and nature that they can receive faith in Christ, and that all who have human nature also have an aptitude to receive this same faith. For it is not to be believed that there would be anyone so ignorant as to think that some end can be attained while the necessary means to it might in no wise be attainable.

Wherefore, as we know, very Truth, Which can neither deceive nor be deceived, in choosing heralds of the faith for the preaching of the word, declared: "Going, teach all nations." Now, by "all," He meant, without any distinction, inasmuch as all have a capacity for the doctrine of the faith.

And invidiously beholding all of this, the Enemy of the same human race, who ever opposes all good human beings in order to destroy them, excogitated an unheard-of method for preventing the Word of God from being preached to the nations that they might be saved: he aroused certain minions of his, who, desirous of satiating their appetites, had the effrontery to declare everywhere that the Western and Southern Indians, and others who have come to Our knowledge in these times, should be reduced to our service, under the pretext that they are without the Catholic Faith, as if they had been irrational animals. And indeed they do so reduce them to slavery, burdening them with toil as they burden the irrational animals that they have at their service.

We, therefore, unworthy Vicar of the same Lord, seeking by every means the return of the sheep of His flock confided to us who have wandered far from the fold, considering that the aforesaid Indians, as true human beings, not only have a capacity for the Christian faith, but, as We know, welcome the same with all alacrity, and desirous of intervening in this matter with appropriate remedies, by the present letters do decree and declare, with Our Apostolic Authority, that the aforesaid Indians and all other peoples who in future may come to Christian cognizance, though they be outside the faith of Christ, must be deprived neither of their freedom nor of the ownership of their goods; indeed, that they may freely and licitly use, possess, and enjoy this liberty and this ownership; nor may they be reduced to slavery; anything to the contrary being illicit, null, and void; and that the aforesaid Indians and other nations must be invited to receive the same faith of Christ by the preaching of the Word and the example of a good life; that copies of these presents, signed by a Notary Public and stamped with the seal of some person in ecclesiastical rank, is to enjoy the same credit as these presents in the original, all previous dispositions or anything else of the kind to the contrary notwithstanding.

Given at Rome, in the Basilica of Saint Peter the Apostle, in the year from the Incarnation of Our Lord one thousand fifteen hundred thirty-seven, on the second day of June, in the third year of Our pontificate.

This document is unequivocal. The pope could not be more clear in his defense of the natives as persons and as free, and therefore as being entitled to the possession of their goods. It is noteworthy that the first intervention of the official magisterium in Latin America was of an unmistakably liberative tenor. Here lie the roots of a tradition that has culminated in our day with the option of the church for the poor, and with the theology of liberation. We only regret that our local churches, and the magisterium itself, have not referred more copiously to this letter — this crystal-clear testimony, amid such complicity on the part of the Iberian church with the conquistadors, to the evangelical attitude of Pope Paul III toward the oppressed.

15 | "Land of True Peace": Las Casas's Peaceful Evangelization

Bartolomé de Las Casas (1474–1566), before ever becoming a Dominican, or bishop of Chiapas, or the great defender of the natives, was an *encomendero* in La Hispaniola (today's Dominican Republic), and the owner of a great many Indian slaves.[16] He arrived there in 1502. In 1510 he heard the famous sermon by Frei Pedro de Córdoba on the situation of the natives. The sermon moved him to conversion, and in 1514 he renounced his lands and became the great defender of the natives. In 1519 and 1520, on the coast of Venezuela, in the company of some good Spanish colonists, he began an expermiment in peaceful coexistence, with the purpose of initiating the natives into the faith and Hispanic culture. He failed, owing to the attempts of other Spaniards to enslave the natives. The natives rebelled, killing some of the missionaries and forcing others to flee. Las Casas retired to the Dominican house in the city of Santo Domingo in 1521. He became a Dominican, and devoted himself to meditation and study until 1529. Thereupon he set off on a five years' journey through Mexico, Honduras, Nicaragua, and other mission regions of the Caribbean, impelled by his concern for the situation of the natives. His famous books, the *Very Brief Account of the Destruction of the Indies*, and the *History of the Indies*, provides us with a record of the violence and cruelty that all but exterminated the natives of these lands.

In 1536 Las Casas set himself to composing a dissertation on missionary method. He called it *On the Only Way to Draw All Peoples to the True Religion*. It was written in elegant Latin, and was replete with citations from the fathers of the church. It is known in Latin as the *De Unico Vocationis Modo*.[17]

Las Casas maintains the following basic thesis:

Divine providence has established one single method alone, for the whole world and for all times, of instructing human beings in the true religion, namely: the persuasion of the understanding by means of reasoning, and the invitation and gentle coaxing of the will. There can be no doubt that this manner ought to be common to the Christian education of all human beings of the world, without the least distinction of sects, errors, or corruption of customs. . . . There is only one way, proper to the divine Wisdom, which delicately, gently, and sweetly provides and moves all created beings to effect their acts and tend toward their natural ends. . . . Accordingly, our manner of instructing human beings in the true doctrine ought to be delicate, gentle, and sweet.[18]

On the basis of this method, Las Casas establishes certain principles to guarantee the genuinely peaceful character of mission. Here are five of them.

First, the evangelized must understand that the missionaries have no wish to dominate them.

Second, the evangelized must be convinced that the missionaries are unmoved by any desire for wealth.

Third, the missionaries must be "so gentle and humble, so affable and meek, so lovable and kindly in speaking with their auditors, and especially with unbelievers, that they arouse in them the will to listen with pleasure and to hold their doctrine in the greatest reverence."

Fourth, preachers must burn with the universal love and charity with which we know Saint Paul to have been consumed, and thereby be led to perform works as extraordinary as his.

Fifth, and finally, preachers must lead such exemplary lives that all persons will be able to see that their preaching is holy and just.

For all these points, Las Casas amassed an impressive argumentation, drawn from Scripture, tradition, and the practice of the church in its evangelization of Spain and England.

Bartolomé de Las Casas did not content himself with theory, although his theory has prevailed intact to our own day. He applied it. He did so in Guatemala, in the so-called Land of War, a territory that had gained its appellation from its reputation for ferocity on the part of human being and beast alike.

Las Casas changed its name to "Land of True Peace." For thirteen years, from 1537 to 1550, the evangelization undertaken there must surely rank as one of the most original in the Christian history of Latin America. Having obtained the required authorization, Las Casas and his three Dominican confreres prepared themselves by fasts and spiritual exercises over a number of days, then they composed a number of tales in verse (called "romances") to convey the tenets of the Christian faith. These they set to music, entrusting them to four Christian Indians who plied their commerce in those inhospitable lands. The four natives memorized the "romances," and betook themselves to the mountains. There they began to sing them, accompanying themselves on native instruments. Within a week they had achieved enormous success, despite their having previously taught that the gods of the natives were idols and the sacrifices they offered them idolatrous and diabolical. When the natives wished to know more, the four merchants told them that only the Dominican fathers, virtuous and peaceful individuals, could teach them. And they returned with an invitation from the Indian chief to come to his lands, while an envoy who had joined the merchants secretly observed the Dominicans to see whether they were indeed virtuous and peaceful.

In response, Las Casas sent a missionary, who was received with great feasting. Then a church was built. The missionary succeeded by his preaching in persuading the natives to tear down their temples and burn their "idols." With the favorable outcome of this second stage of the project, other Dominicans now visited this erstwhile Land of War, Las Casas among them. Years passed, and the peaceful mission prospered. Las Casas, with this example, and with his fine rhetoric, obtained numerous decrees from the Spanish monarchs in behalf of the Indians, especially from 1540 onward. Meanwhile, in the rest of Guatemala, colonists strove by every means to belittle this experiment and cut short its continuation.

In 1544 Las Casas was appointed Bishop of Chiapas, a territory that included the Land of True Peace. In response to the pressures exerted by the colonists, he began imposing outright excommunication on the most highly placed of them, who had come into the native territories to subjugate the inhabitants. In

1550, at the age of seventy-six, worn out with toil and sorrow, he resigned his episcopal office.

Las Casas's experiment finished in tragedy. A letter of May 14, 1556, from the surviving Dominicans to the Council of the Indies, tells of the end.[19] Despite all difficulties, the Dominican missioners had toiled with great fervor, "destroying idols, burning temples, erecting churches, and gaining souls." Meanwhile, native priests, allying themselves with others who had not been converted, incited a rebellion. The missioners were expelled: two were killed in their church, one was sacrificed to an "idol," and thirty native Christians were shot to death with arrows. When the missionaries sent for help, their fellow-Spaniards ignored them, claiming they had no authority to enter the native territories. Later the King of Spain dispatched a punitive expedition, forcing the natives into subjection. And the attempt at a peaceful evangelization had met its tragic end.

In critical retrospect, we must look for the Achilles' heel in this so-called peaceful strategy. Actually, it was not peaceful enough. There is a considerable dose of violence at its heart — not physical violence, to be sure, but another type of violence, which also destroys: symbolical violence. The religion of the natives went unacknowledged. The validity of their store of religious images was not accepted. The destruction of their "idols" was decreed by fire and sword. Their priests and shamans were persecuted.[20] Today we know from anthropology that religion is the very heart of culture, and we have seen this above. It is its soul, and most radical meaning. But to destroy the heart of a culture is tantamount to beheading a community, or to tearing the skeleton out of its body, and thereby decreeing the cultural death of a people. Tragically, this is what happened to the "witness cultures" of Latin America, as well as to the black nations kidnapped and shipped there as merchandise.

At the basis of this strategy of symbolical violence (a consequence of the narrow Christian dogmatism of those days), the Christianity that was implanted on the Latin American continent was without authentic cultural roots. It was part of the project of incorporation of the natives into the Iberian universe, and into a single, stereotyped European Christendom. The historical opportunity to create, in the tropics, a Christianity culturally distinct from the West European, was lost.

16 | The Liberative Method of the Dark Virgin

The conditions for a liberative and typical Latin American Christianity, fruit of a new evangelization and of an intercultural encounter, were already present in the sixteenth century, when Spanish colonialism was consolidated and the yearning for life and liberty arose on the part of natives. I refer to the apparition of the dark Virgin of Guadalupe, who is still today the most powerful religious and popular reference of the Latin American peoples. I do not intend to discuss the critical aspects of the presumed event of Mary's apparition to a Nahuatl native. I take the event as it is experienced by those who profess faith in it and as accepted by the official church. But I am especially interested in the method that can be deduced from that faith event. There is a liberative method there, and one that interrelates all the internal and external elements of the apparition.

MISSING: A DIALOGUE BETWEEN GOSPEL AND NATIVE RELIGION

In order to understand the novelty of the evangelizing method of Our Lady of Guadalupe, we must consider the extent to which Aztec civilization was being destroyed under Spanish domination. Let us recall certain dates. On April 22, 1519, began the long Good Friday of the agony and death of Mexican culture, as Hernando Cortés disembarked on the Mexican coast with 600 soldiers, 16 horses, and a few pieces of artillery. On August 13, 1521, after a long siege, Tenochtitlán, the Aztec capital, fell. It is calculated that 240,000 warriors died.

The anonymous Tlaltelolco Document (written in Nahuatl around 1528) records the awful scene:

Along the routes lie broken arrows, hair is scattered about, tiles have been blasted from the houses, walls are ablaze. Worms abound in streets and squares, and the walls are splotched with blown-out brains. . . . We have eaten grass covered with saltpeter, pieces of clay, lizards, rats, dust, and even the worms.[21]

The Aztecs believed that their own defeat meant the defeat of their male and female divinities. A mournful hymn dating from 1523 acknowledges: "Weep, my friends! Know that, with these happenings, we lose the Mexican nation. The water has gone bitter, the food has gone bitter. Behold the deed of the Giver of Life in Tlaltelolco!"[22]

In the celebrated Dialogue of the Twelve Apostles (the first Franciscan missioners, who arrived in 1524) with the Aztec sages in 1525, the case is clear: "Where are we to go? We are simple folk, we are perishable, we are mortal. Let us die, then, let us perish, for our Gods themselves have died."[23] And in agony and despair, the Aztec nation died.

On December 9, 1531, ten years after the defeat of Motecuhzoma, Our Lady appeared on Mount Tepeyac, on the outskirts of the capital, where Tonantzin, the "Worshipful Mother," was venerated. She appeared to Juan Diego, an Aztec native who was learning his catechism in Tlaltelolco. I need not describe all the events — the apparition, the Virgin Mother's message to Bishop Juan de Zumárraga, the construction of the temple dedicated to Mary in Tepeyac. Let us attend only to the elements that bear on our theme of evangelization as a method of encounter between culture and gospel.

First, Our Lady appears with a mestizo face, symbolizing the encounter between Spanish and natives — but with priority assigned to the native contribution, since she appears to one of them, and adopts the symbols of their culture.[24]

Second, she speaks not in Spanish, but in Nahuatl, the language of the Aztecs. She speaks in the religious style reserved by the Aztecs for God: "I am the Mother of the most true God, by whom is life, the creator of persons, the Lord of the near and immediate, Sovereign of sky and earth." She makes her appearance unifying the masculine (the sun) and the feminine (the moon and stars), as did the Aztecs, whose divinities were always androgynous. Mario Rojas has shown that, in the ancient Aztec religion, the expression "Mother of God" or "Our Mother" translates the feminine aspect of the deity—God with the face of a mother. Indeed, the Virgin Mother of Guadalupe appears upon the sun, enveloped in its rays, with the moon below, and a mantle of stars, which some say correspond to the position of the stars in the days of her apparitions in Tepeyac.

The sun and moon were the great Aztec deities. Mary subsumes both in herself. Her tunic is of the color of Huitzilopochtli, the supreme god, the god of life, pale red—the color of the east, as well, reborn victoriously each morning after having passed through the mortal risks of night. Juan Diego later understood this color to be that of the blood offered daily by the Aztecs to keep the sun alive, that it might continue to give life to all living beings. The flowers adorning the tunic are the flowers of Tepeyac, where the Mother-God was worshiped. The mantle is of blue and green, the colors of the divinities of sky (blue) and fertile earth (green). Among the Aztecs, only the king and the divinity might wear these two colors in combination.

Mary appears as pregnant, wearing the symbols that Aztec women wore over their abdomens, two low black belts. Next to them she wears a little native cross (*quincunce*), which for the Aztecs signified the crossroads of human beings and the gods. It is like a four-petaled rose (the human beings' road) with a circle in the center (the gods' road). This basic symbol of Aztec culture is on Mary's abdomen, as if to say: what she bears in her womb, what will be born, is the encounter between God and human beings, Jesus. At the same time, at the center of the collar of her robe, at the Virgin Mother's neck, is the Christian cross, as if to say: now a part of Aztec culture, she yet remains the Mother of the Son who was crucified for our liberation. The angel, whose wings are those of a bird that lives in the Mexican tropics (*tzinitzcan*), who bears the Blessed Mother aloft, signifies the divine origin of the one now making her appearance. And indeed, according to the Aztec calendar (as on the famous Sun Stone), every important era was ushered in by a celestial being. Thus, Mary symbolizes the new age of salvation through Jesus and through the Spirit who engenders Jesus in Mary's womb.

Here she is the vessel of both: of the eternal Son, in her womb, and of the Spirit, who is creating for him, of Mary, a human nature.

FROM THE CENTER TO THE PERIPHERY

To whom does Mary appear? Not to a Spaniard, or to anyone representing the institutional church. She appears to a marginalized native. The Virgin Mother herself says, in her first self-communication to him: "Juanito, my child, who should have been treated with supreme respect, but who are marginalized — where are you going?" The conquistadors dealt very harshly with the Aztecs. Juan Diego had introjected the negative image of the natives that they had created. He recognizes himself as a "poor little Indian," a country bumpkin, a despicable thing, a withered leaf on a tree. ("I am a Mecapal, I am a Parihuela, I am offal. Alas, I am a little Indian.") In Europe, with its pyramidal feudal aristocracy, Mary is called Our Lady, or addressed with similar honorific titles. In Latin America, she tells Juan Diego, she wishes to be called "Girl, Young Virgin, Little Girl, Young Daughter Mine, Miss," and "Compassionate Mother of the People." She takes her place in the affective and linguistic universe of the people, and of the poor. She makes an option for the impoverished, degraded Indians.

Mary takes a place on the periphery, and not in the center.[25] She does not speak from Bishop Zumárraga's palace, in the capital, built with materials from the destroyed Aztec pyramids. She speaks from Tepeyac, in an outlying district of scant importance. She chooses Juan Diego, whom she affectionately calls "Juanito" or "Dieguito" — the poor little Indian, as the Spaniards would have called him. The native, subjugated by the conquistadors, is to evangelize the bishop, a person of high rank in the center. He goes not with violence, as the Spaniards have come to the Aztecs, but with words of conviction, and finally, with flowers that he carries in his poncho and casts at the bishop's feet.

The evangelizing mission of Juan Diego reminds us of the words of Puebla concerning the "evangelizing potential of the poor" (Puebla Final Document, no. 1147). The message that the Blessed Virgin sends the bishop implies a shift from the center to the periphery: she asks that a temple be built at Tepeyac, where she wishes to make "God [known] to the nations, in all my personal love, in my compassionate glance, in my aid, in my salvation, for I am in truth your compassionate mother." Mary reveals her mission to the poor: "Here I desire to hear your laments, and to come to your assistance in your pain and sorrow." The apparition, and the mission entrusted to Juan Diego for implementation by the bishop of the dominators, reveals a new meaning of evangelization. Evangelization is no longer institutional, originating with power above the Indians and exercised for them by others. This is an evangelization that begins with the poor and is open to all.

When we start from the seat of power, we suppose that the natives are ignorant ne'er-do-wells. Evangelization communicates a particular content to them: they are the object of the activity of one group upon another. And it is this that is supposed to lead them to act and to live in a Christian manner. Evangelization that starts from the people involves everyone, as Our Lady of Guadalupe shows. Both Juan Diego and Bishop Zumárraga must hear the Virgin's message, move from their accustomed surroundings, and attend to the poor, whom Mary seeks to console. Evangelization will not be the spread of the church system, but the creation of communities around a message.

All are invited by Mary to leave the center, Tenochtitlan-Tlaltelolco, and transport themselves to the periphery in Tepeyac. The journey will allow persons and institutions to undergo an Abrahamic experience, and to be evangelized by living with the poor and generating for them good news of life and salvation.

The figure of Juan Diego's uncle, called Juan Bernardino, is interesting. He is ill, and on the edge of death. Our Lady of Guadalupe heals him. In Aztec culture the uncle is a most respected figure. His legacy goes not to his children, but to his nephews. He symbolizes the nation. Here he is ill, prostrate with all the Aztec nation. Then with Guadalupe he bestirs himself and returns to life. This is the good news that Mary brings the native culture. It is the native gospel of liberation. The Aztecs understand the whole language — Our Lady's words, her symbols, the importance of Juan Diego and his uncle Juan Bernardino. They are converted en masse. The hopes of a people live once more. The divinities have not died! Now, under the figure of the Virgin Mother of Tepeyac, comes salvation, the strength to resist, and courage for liberation.

We may conclude: the Latin American church has yet to learn the lesson of Guadalupe. It must overcome a pietistic, merely ecclesiastical interpretation. It must attend to all the elements. There is a lesson to be drawn here: it is possible to be fully Aztec and to be a Christian at the same time. The Virgin Mother has shown us this. It is important that we extend the creative method of Guadalupe: only then shall we have an evangelization under the sign of liberation — an evangelization that will engender an Amerindian Catholic Church on this continent.

Conclusion:
Building a Culture
of Life and Freedom Together

After all these reflections on the relationship between evangelization and cultures, and the essential evangelizing methodology, it is time to order to summarize our basic perspectives in a number of propositions.

1. Puebla has mapped out the correct route by which we may execute an authentic evangelization today. To cite, once more, the Puebla Final Document:

> The Church has been acquiring an increasingly clear and deep realization that evangelization is its fundamental mission; and that it cannot possibly carry out this mission without an ongoing effort to know the real situation and to adapt the gospel message to today's human beings in a dynamic, attractive, and convincing way. [no. 85]

What is asserted here is that the good news is produced from an encounter between concrete reality and the Christian message. It will not be enough to propagate this message as it was once codified in history. That may guarantee the orthodoxy of the propositions, but it will not ensure the character of the message as good news that actually helps persons. That character depends on the reality to be analyzed, time and again, in our searches, failures, and successes, and confronted with Jesus' utopic project. The historico-social reality of the Latin American peoples is characterized by immense hopes, awash in a sea of oppression. The entire social fabric is shot through with oppressed cultures, humiliated races, exploited classes, and marginalized peripheries. At the same time, the oppressed are mobilizing: in a thousand ways, the downtrodden are raising their consciousness, organizing, resisting, and striving to advance in the direction of their freedom. Faced with this antireality of oppressed cultures, the church no longer has any relevant option but the option for the cultures of the oppressed and marginalized, with a view to their liberation.

2. The base Christian communities are situated within this process of resistance and liberation. They are part of the social movement. They have managed to burst the bonds of subjection in which the Christian churches have suffered in the capitalist order. Historically, the churches, especially the Roman Catholic Church, have been more involved with the interests of the organizers of this order, which marginalizes the great majorities, than with members of the subordinate strata of the population. It continues to be the great merit of Christians committed to social transformations through movements like the base church communities, bible circles, alternative health cooperatives, human rights groups, groups of landless, homeless, of marginalized women and others, to have extracted the liberative dimension of Jesus' message for the oppressed of our society.

3. In these circles, the new evangelization is under way. It is new in many ways. It is based on the *gospel* rather than on the pure and simple propagation of church doctrine. The people read the gospel together, in communities, interpreting it in an atmosphere of prayer and communion, and living it by applying it to the problems of the popular culture. It is here that the gospel appears as the good news of liberation.

It is a new evangelization in that its *principal subject* and agent are the poor themselves. The novelty here is that the poor are evangelizing other poor; and, as poor, evangelizing the whole church. It is a new evangelization in that it has *new addressees*, such as popular culture and piety, blacks, marginalized women (for example, prostitutes), street children, the chronically sick, the landless, the homeless, slum dwellers, and so on. It is new in that it employs *new methods*, along the lines of the pedagogy of the oppressed, and of education as a practice of freedom, of the famous Christian educator Paulo Freire, according to whom educand and educator, catechized and catechist, enter into a process of mutual apprenticeship and exchange of learning, on the basis of accumulated experience, which is criticized and broadened in an integral perspective that attends to the various dimensions of personal, social, intellectual, affective, cultural, and religious human existence.

It is new in that it communicates *new content*, derived from an interrelationship between the discourse of faith and the discourse of the world of the oppressed. It discovers that, in biblical revelation, there is an essential bond between the God of life, the poor, and liberation, between the reign of God, which first comes into being among the impoverished, and the politico-social dimension of life and the ultimate sense of history—always in a dialectical relationship with the anti-reign, which is also structured in history, occasioning martyrdom, manipulation of the name of God, and oppressions of every order.

It is new in that it inaugurates a *new way of being church*. It is characterized by community, a participation offered to all, a distribution of functions, the emergence of new ministries and charisms, and the new kind of Christian, emerging through sharing in community and society, and through striking solidarity with other oppressed persons, to social transformations that objectify a new kind of coexistence.

It is new in that it generates a *new spirituality*, which appears in celebrations not only of the mysteries of faith, but of the struggles and joys of the community. It appears in the manner of its political commitment to collective causes concerned with the poor and outcast, in the new social holiness woven of testimonials of solidarity, persecution, and martyrs.

It is new in that it forges a *new relation of church to world*: a relation that is no longer an alliance of the church with the powerful, but is a relationship of participation, and support for the oppressed sectors of society, a relationship that takes up the defense of the rights of the poor, and mounts an intransigent campaign of protection and promotion of the life of the groups threatened with death, like those evicted from their land, the natives, and other outcasts. The prevailing Latin American order knows that, in the local and regional churches that take their preferential option for the poor seriously, it is facing an ally of the organized people, and a champion of a liberation whose goal is a new, more participatory and just, society.

4. The evangelization of Latin America took place under the sign of colonialism. Thus, just as the factories and structures copied from the metropolis were set up here, so also a religious structure was designed that was to guarantee faith and salvation by itself. For the prevailing understanding of the missionaries, an understanding shared by the theology of the age, the creation of a visible church was a *sine qua non* of faith and salvation: the church, in its visibility, was the sacrament necessary for salvation, and was possessed of all the means of faith and salvation that converts would ever need. This was the main thing. The accent did not fall on the generation of the new man and woman. To be sure, a conversion as change in life was sought. Basically, however, this was the task of the individual convert. The important thing was that the means of holiness and salvation be available to all institutionally.

The new evangelization takes a different tack. It is less eager for the creation of religious institutions than for the emergence of new Christians, Christians who live the aspect of salvation that imitates the divine Trinity of communion, in an ethic of the following of Jesus and in a life according to the Spirit. This route is the foundation of a communitarian Christianity. Here, persons are in direct confrontation with their needs, opportunities, and internal potential. Communitarian Christianity, fruit of the new evangelization, rests on "witness persons" far more than on institutions. Therefore it is more like a movement than like organized power. So it is more like the movement of Jesus and the apostles than the ecclesiastical structurization that began in the third century and has predominated in conventional Christianity down to our own day, under the hegemony of the clergy. The links between the church communities (already interlinked) with other movements heading in the same direction (pastoral ministry of the land, of natives, of women, of human rights, and so on) concretely constitute the people of God. This theological category—the people of God—ceases to be a metaphor, and becomes the literal description of an observable phenomenon: the people of God, of the poor, the tissue of interlinked base communities, are historical realities in society, and today are the bearers of the liberating message of Jesus in the midst of the oppressed. Along with other movements, they make up the historical bloc that seeks a new society.

5. The presence of the new way of being church in society is characterized by the will to service rather than to power. Evangelization is no longer married to the societal establishment, sharing in its hegemonic power, as was the case in the colonial era and up to the 1960s. This participation enabled the local and regional churches to create a vast network of services to the poor. It made for a beneficent church. But this church was not a participatory one. It attended to the wants of the poor, but it did not school them to liberate themselves from their dependency and to become subjects, agents, of their own situation.

Today, via the network of base communities, the people are learning to be active subjects of their church and their social situation. They also learn to see history from the viewpoint of their own condition as oppressed, and discover the transforming potential of the underside of history. This is especially so when they realize that God is on their side, and that Jesus' plan implies an integral liberation, one that includes economic, political and social — in a word, a cultural — liberation.

6. This liberative dimension of evangelization emerges only if we place ourselves in the position Jesus took. Jesus was on the side of the last, the left out, those on the seamy side of history. To evangelize cultures, then, means to begin with the oppressed and outcast cultures, and from there to seek to understand why the dominating cultures exist, and how they must be reached by the gospel message, that they may cease to be oppressive. Together with other cultures, they may come to constitute constructive forces of a humanity of coexistence and community, in a democracy that includes a cosmos whose elements are regarded and respected as sisters and brothers.

7. Evangelization must always be integral. But to guarantee its character as good news, and to respond to the challenges of an oppressed cultural reality, it must basically be aimed at defense of the life and culture of the poor. It is not the place of the churches to wield the hegemony of the cultural process. The churches must associate themselves with other social actors striving for the same objectives and following the same or similar methods in quest of the constitution of a historical subject capa-

ble of building a different society, a more livable society of universal fellowship. Our churches must lend their collaboration in a process that transcends them historically and theologically. The new society abuilding is caught up in the historical design of God, and endowed with the signs of the reign of God in this world. Christians are not the only laborers on this construction site. Together with other daughters and sons of God, they find themselves under the same Light that enlightens every human being who comes into the world, and indwelt by the same Strength who dwells within everyone walking the road that leads to the Father.

Notes

PREFACE

1. See the commentary and collection of studies by José Ramos Regidor, "500 anni d'invasione dell'America Latina," *Emergenze*, June 1988.

2. Cf. Aloísio Lorscheider, "Nova evangelização e vida religiosa," *Irmão Sol*, December 1988, pp. 2–3.

3. Cf. Robert Jaulín, comp., *El etnocidio a través de las Américas* (Mexico City, 1976), esp. pp. 55–56; P. Chaunu, *Conquista e exploração dos novos mundos* (São Paulo, 1984), p. 404; Gustavo Gutiérrez, *Dios o el oro en las Indias, siglo XVI* (Lima, 1989), pp. 10, 42–47.

4. T. Todorov, *A conquista da América: a questão do otro* (São Paulo, 1988), p. 129.

5. Cf. G. Girardi, *La conquista de América: Con qué derecho?* (San José, Costa Rica: DEI, 1988), pp. 17–34.

6. See Rubén Darío García, comp., "Evangelización y liberación en la historia latinoamericana," in *Evangelización y liberación*, by various authors (Buenos Aires, 1986), pp. 56–57.

PART 1. EVANGELIZING FROM OPPRESSED CULTURES

1. See certain more general works: José Comblin, "Evangelizéción de la cultura en América Latina," *Puebla* 2 (1978): 91–109; Pedro Trigo, "Evangelización de la cultura," *Puebla* 5 (1979): 298–303; P. Suess, "Inculturação: desafios—caminhos—metas," *Revista Eclesiástica Brasileira* 49 (1989): 81–126; idem, "Cultura e religião," ibid., pp. 778–98.

2. See the most significant titles in this line: CNBB/CIMI, *Inculturação e libertação* (São Paulo: Paulinas, 1986; CRB, *Nova evangelização e vida religiosa no Brasil* (Rio de Janeiro, 1989); M. Azevedo, *Comunidades eclesiais de base e inculturação da fé* (São Paulo: Loyola, 1986); idem, *Inculturação e libertação* (São Paulo: Loyola, 1986); idem, "Evangelización inculturada," *Misiones Extranjeras* 87 (1985): 197–221; J. M. de Paiva, *Colonização e catequese* (São Paulo: Cortez, 1982); ILADES, *Cultura y evangelización en América Latina* (Santiago: Paulinas, 1988); various authors, *Evangelización y liberación* (Buenos Aires:

Paulinas, 1986); various authors, *Evangelización de la cultura e incul-turación del evangelio* (Buenos Aires: Guadalupe, 1989); F. Damen, *Hacia una teología de la inculturación* (La Paz: Conferencia Boliviana de Religiosos, 1989); the entire no. 196 (1989) of *Revista Eclesiástica Brasileira: Evangelização e Cultura*.

3. See certain more general works: R. de Barros Laraia, *Cultura: um conceito antropológico* (Rio de Janeiro: Zahar, 1986; D. Kaplan and R. A. Manners, *Teoria da cultura* (Rio de Janeiro: Zahar, 1978; C. Geertz, *The Interpretation of Cultures* (New York: Basic Books, 1973); B. Malinowski, *Une théorie scientifique de la culture* (Paris: Maspero, 1968); C. Lévi-Strauss, *Race and History* (Paris: UNESCO, 1968); P. Menezes, "As origens da cultura," *Sintese* 15 (1988): 13–24; Darcy Ribeiro, *O processo civilizatório* (Petrópolis, Vozes, 1983); C. R. Brandão, "Impor, persuadir, convidar, dialogar: a cultura do outro," in *Inculturação e libertação* (Paulinas), pp. 9–26; idem, *A arca de Noé: Algumas anotações sobre sentidos e diferenças a respeito da idéia de cultura e novos desafios à evangelização da América Latina*, forthcoming from Vozes (Petrópolis); also very clear is the work of P. Suess cited above: "Inculturação: desafios — caminhos — metas" (n. 1).

4. The description by the Vatican II *Gaudium et Spes* (no. 53) reveals the overarching nature of culture.

5. Marxism-Leninism is formally atheistic, and organized the state in lay fashion, without any explicit reference to religion. Meanwhile, it constructed a complex of social symbols, focused on revolution and its superstars (for example, the personage of Lenin, with his mausoleum in the Kremlin), with the religious characters of respect, ultimate reality, veneration — attitudes that culturally had been reserved to the supreme value, God.

6. Cf. M. Azevedo, *Evangelización de la cultura e inculturación del evangelio* (Buenos Aires, 1988); P. Suess, "Inculturação: desafios — caminhos — metas," *Revista Eclesiástica Brasileira* 49 (1989): 95–97; N. Standaert, "L'histoire d'un néologisme: Le terme 'inculturation' dans les documents romains," *Nouvelle Revue Théologique* 110 (1988): 555–70.

7. O. Ianni, *Raças e classes sociais no Brasil* (Rio de Janeiro, 1966), p. 27; C. Prado Júnior, *Formação do Brasil contemporaneo* (São Paulo, 1963), pp. 16–17; Darcy Ribeiro, *La cultura latinoamericana, Cuadernos de cultura latinoamericana* (Mexico City, 1978).

8. F. Mires, *La colonización de las almas* (San José, Costa Rica: DEI, 1987); A. Marquínez, *Ideología y praxis de la conquista* (Bogotá, 1978); Gustavo Gutiérrez, *Dios o el oro en las Indias, siglo XVI* (Lima: CEP, 1989). See the two classics on the subject: R. Ricard, *La conquista espiritual de México* (Mexico City, 1986); Lewis Hanke, *Colonisation et*

conscience chrétienne au XVI siècle (Paris: Plon, 1957).

9. See the book written in 1570 by Juan Focher, O.F.M. (d. 1572), a *vade mecum* of missioners who came to America. In various places, it defends the just war against the heathen, that is, the natives: *Itinerario del misionero en América* (Madrid, 1960), part 1, chap. 5, 11; part 3, chap. 1-7.

10. On the publication of these catechisms, see J. Guillermo Durán, *Monumenta catechetica hispanoamericana*, vol. 1 (Buenos Aires, 1984).

11. Cf. *Los coloquios de los doce apóstoles*, in Durán, *Monumenta*, p. 215.

12. Ibid., p. 187.

13. Ibid., pp. 93, 164.

14. Ibid., p. 228.

15. *Cartas dos primeiros jesuítas do Brasil*, vol. 2 (Rio de Janeiro, 1938), p. 27.

16. Ibid., p. 379.

17. See the important study by J. O. Beozzo, "Visão indígena da conquista e da evangelização," in *Inculturação e libertação* (Paulinas), pp. 79-104.

18. Cf. E. Hoornaert, *O catolicismo moreno* (Petrópolis, Brazil: Vozes, 1990).

19. Vatican II well says that "God has spoken in accordance with the particular culture of various ages" (*Gaudium et Spes*, no. 58; cf. no. 44).

20. The fact of Jesus' new life was interpreted in the primitive church through two distinct categories: that of the elevation/exaltation of the suffering just one (of apocalyptical origin), and that of the resurrection (of eschatological origin). These were two distinct cultural codes, used to express the novelty of the fact of the crucified one's now being alive in an altogether unique manner (Paul calls Christ the *novissimus Adam*, with a spiritual body — 1 Cor. 15:44). It is not a matter of the reanimation of a corpse, as with Lazarus, but of a full glorification and transfiguration of Jesus' earthly reality, in its entirety, in its corporeality and its spirituality. For this entire question, see J. Kremer, *Die Osterbotschaft der vier Evangelien* (Stuttgart, 1968); idem, *Das älteste Zeugnis von der Auferstehung Christi* (Stuttgart, 1967); P. Seidensticker, *Die Auferstehung Jesu in der Botschaft der Evangelien* (Stuttgart, 1968); Leonardo Boff, *A ressurreição de Cristo — a nossa ressurreição na morte* (Petrópolis, Vozes, 1976).

21. See, for example, R. Schnackenburg, "A ressurreição de Jesus Cristo como ponto de partida e de apoio da cristologia neotestamentária," in *Mysterium Salutis*, vol. 3/2 (Petrópolis: Vozes, 1973), pp. 8-23.

22. Cf. M. Fang, "Teología de la inculturación," in *Evangelización de la cultura*, by various authors, pp. 201–25, esp. 210.

23. Vatican II expresses the sense of this assumption: The "purpose" of the church "has been to adapt the gospel to the grasp of all as well as to the needs of the learned, insofar as such was appropriate. Indeed, this accommodated preaching of the revealed Word ought to remain the law of all evangelization. For thus each nation develops the ability to express Christ's message in its own way" (*Gaudium et Spes*, no. 44).

24. Vatican II states, concerning the anthropological-transcultural meaning of Christ: "The Lord is the goal of human history, the focal point of the longings of history and of civilization, the center of the human race, the joy of every heart, and the answer to all its yearnings. He it is whom the Father raised from the dead, lifted on high, and stationed at His right hand, making Him Judge of the living and the dead" (ibid., no. 45).

25. The first text written in Latin America, in 1498, was that of Fray Ramón Pané, *Relación acerca de las antigüedades de los indios*, republished in Mexico City in 1985. Already the religions of the natives were being referred to in a negative, satanizing way (pp. 21, 35, 41).

26. See the critical essays of Catholic historian J. Delumeau, "Quelle église pour faire l'évangile?" *Témoinage Chrétien*, August 21–27, 1989. See also the pertinent observations of Spanish theologian J. I. González Faus, "El meollo de la involución eclesial," *Razón y Fe*, July-August 1989, pp. 57–84.

27. The first two references are titles of books by the famous Brazilian educator Paulo Freire; the last is to Clodovis Boff, *Como trabalhar com o povo* (Petrópolis: Vozes, 1987).

PART 2. MINIMUM CONTENT FOR A NEW EVANGELIZATION

1. See J. M. de Paiva, *Colonização e catequese* (São Paulo, 1982), esp. pp. 41–46.

2. *Cartas dos primeiros jesuitas do Brazil* (São Paulo, 1954), 2:82.

3. Ibid., 3:476.

4. S. Leite, *Novas Cartas jesuíticas* (Rio de Janeiro, 1940), p. 164.

5. Joseph de Anchieta, *Cartas, Informaçãoes, Fragmentos históricos do Pe. Joseph de Anchieta* (Rio de Janeiro, 1933), p. 179.

6. J. Hoeffner, *La ética colonial española del siglo de oro: Cristianismo y dignidad humana* (Madrid, 1957), p. 176.

7. See texts in M. da Nóbrega, *Cartas do Brasil e mais escritos* (Coimbra, 1955), p. 56; see also L. F. Baeta Neves, *O combate dos*

soldados de Cristo na terra dos papagaios: Colonialismo e repressão cultural (Rio de Janeiro, 1978), pp. 93–94.

8. See J. B. Lessègue, *La longa marcha de las Casas* (Lima, 1974), pp. 363–64, 385–86.

9. See Enrique Dussel, *Desintegración de la cristiandad colonial y liberación* (Salamanca, 1978).

10. John Paul II, homily at the Palafoxian Seminary in Puebla, January 28, 1979, no. 2, included in the Puebla volume (Petrópolis: Vozes, 1979), p. 46.

11. See Leonardo Boff, *Trinity and Society* (Tunbridge Wells: Burns and Oates and Maryknoll: Orbis, 1988), pp. 123–54.

12. See Puebla Final Document, no. 212: "Christ reveals to us that the divine life is trinitarian communion. Father, Son, and Spirit live the supreme mystery of oneness in perfect, loving intercommunion. It is the source of all love and all other communion that gives dignity and grandeur to human existence."

13. See Saint Justin, *Apologia* 1 46:1–4; *Apologia* 2 7:1–4, 13:3–4; Clement of Alexandria, *Stromata*, I, 19:91–94; Vatican Council II, *Ad Gentes*, no. 11; *Lumen Gentium*, no. 17.

14. Paul VI, *Evangelii Nuntiandi*, no. 53; Medellín, *Pastoral Popular*, no. 5.

15. See P. Suess, "Questionamentos e perspectivas a partir da causa indígena," in *Inculturação e Libertação*, by various authors (São Paulo, 1986), pp. 160–75; idem, "Culturas indígenas e evangelização," *Revista Eclesiástica Brasileira* 41 (1981): 211–49; R. Nebel, *Altmexikanische Religion und christliche Botschaft: Mexico zwischen Quetzalcóatl und Christus* (Innensee, 1983), pp. 309–68.

16. See A. Antoniazzi, "Encarnação e salvação," in *Inculturação e Libertação*, pp. 130–43.

17. See J. Strieder, "Evangelização e Palavra de Deus," in *Evangelização no Brasil de hoje* (São Paulo, 1976), pp. 75–94.

18. See Jorge Pixley and Clodovis Boff, *The Bible, the Church, and the Poor* (Tunbridge Wells: Burns and Oates and Maryknoll: Orbis, 1989), pp. 53–67.

19. Victorio Araya, *God of the Poor* (Maryknoll, N.Y.: Orbis, 1987).

20. C. Bravo, *Jesús, hombre en conflicto* (Mexico City, 1986), esp. pp. 217–18.

21. See José Comblin, *The Meaning of Mission* (Maryknoll, N.Y.: Orbis Books, 1977).

22. For all this chapter, see José Comblin, *O Espírito Santo e sua missão* (São Paulo, 1984); idem, *The Holy Spirit and Liberation* (Tunbridge Wells: Burns and Oates and Maryknoll, N.Y.: Orbis 1989); idem,

O tempo da ação: Ensaio sobre o Espírito Santo e a história (Petrópolis: 1982); Yves M.-J. Congar, *I Believe in the Holy Sprit* (New York and London, 1983).

23. See Leonardo Boff, "A Igreja, sacramento do Espírito Santo," in *O Espírito Santo: Pessoa, presença atuação*, by various authors (Petrópolis: 1973), pp. 108–25.

24. This is the basic thesis defended in my *Ecclesiogenesis: The Base Communities Reinvent the Church* (Maryknoll, N.Y.: Orbis, 1986), pp. 12–20.

25. See J. Oscar Beozzo, "Para uma liturgia de rosto latino-americano," in *Revista Eclesiástica Brasileira* 49 (1989): 586–605.

26. See the meticulous study by idem, "Visão indígena da conquista e da evangelização," in *Inculturação e Libertação*, pp. 79–104.

27. By way of more readily accessible works, see J. Lafaye, *Quetzalcóatl y Guadalupe* (Mexico City, Madrid, and Buenos Aires: Fondo de Cultura Económica, 1977); V. Elizondo, *La morenita: Evangelización de las Américas* (St. Louis, Mo.: Liguori, 1981); S. Carrillo, *El mensaje teológico de Guadalupe, Nuestra Señora de América*, nos. 14–15 (Bogotá: CELAM, 1986); M. Concha Malo, "La vírgen de Guadalupe y el nacionalismo mexicano desde las clases populares," in *Hacia el nuevo Milenio* (Mexico City, 1986, pp. 107–24); P. Canova, *Guadalupe dalla parte degli ultimi: Storia e messagio* (Vicenza, 1984); C. Siller, *El método de la Evangelización en el Nican Mopohua* (Mexico City, 1986); A. Junco, *Un radical problema guadalupano* (Mexico City, 1971).

PART 3. THE LIBERATIVE METHOD OF OUR LADY OF GUADALUPE

1. See P. Borges, *Métodos misionales en la cristianización de América, siglo XVI* (Madrid: Departamento de Misionología Española, 1960); J. Specker, *Die Missionsmethode in Spanisch-Amerika im 16. Jahrhundert* (Freiburg, 1953); R. Ricard, *La conquista espiritual de México* (Mexico City: Fondo de Cultura Económica, 1986; R. Romano, *Les mécanismes de la conquête coloniale: Les conquistadores* (Paris: Flammarion, 1972); M. de Carcer y Disdier, *Apuntes para la historia de la transculturación indoespañola* (Mexico City, 1953); Lewis Hanke, *The Spanish Struggle for Justice in the Conquest of America* (Philadelphia, 1949).

2. Cf. Ricard, *Conquista espiritual de México*, p. 417.

3. Published in *Cartas do Brasil (1549–1560)* (São Paulo: Itatiaia, 1988), pp. 229–45.

4. José de Acosta, *De Procuranda Indorum Salute*, Biblioteca de autores españoles, 73 (Madrid, 1954).

5. Ibid., book 2, chap. 8, pp. 442–44.

6. Ibid., p. 450.

7. Ibid.

8. Ibid., chap. 8, p. 442. On p. 450 he says: "The soldier and the priest must walk together." Later, on p. 453, he asserts the need to "proclaim the gospel in a new way, surrounded by soldiers and sundry paraphernalia."

9. Cited by Lewis Hanke in the Introduction to Bartolomé de Las Casas, *Del único modo de atraer a todos los pueblos a la verdadera religión* (Mexico City: Fondo de Cultura Económica, 1975), p. 59.

10. See the analysis of the various methods in Borges, *Métodos misionales*, pp. 250–455.

11. A good analysis of the various initiatives will be found in Lewis Hanke, *Colonisation et conscience chrétienne au XVI siècle* (Paris: Plon, 1957), pp. 100–119.

12. Vol. 1, p. 139.

13. Cited by Hanke, *Del único modo*, p. 28.

14. See Hanke's study, "The Requirement and Its Interpreters" *Revista Historia de America* (Mexico City, 1938) and *Revista do Brasil*, September 1938, pp. 231–48.

15. Las Casas, *Del único modo*, pp. 322–24.

16. There is a great deal of literature on Las Casas. See, e.g., Enrique Dussel, "Bartolomeu de Las Casas no quinto centenário de seu nascimento," in *Caminhos de libertação latino-americana*, vol. 2 (São Paulo: Paulinas, 1985), pp. 135–55.

17. I shall cite the recent edition (Mexico City: Fondo de Cultura Económica, 1975); see also Hanke's remarkable introduction, with its history of the experiment in peaceful evangelization in the land of true peace, pp. 21–60.

18. Las Casas, *Del único modo*, book 5, no. 1, pp. 65–66; cf. p. 67.

19. See Hanke, *Del único modo*, pp. 52–53.

20. The missionaries were seized with a mighty, destructive frenzy when it came to temples and "idols," especially in Mexico. Mexico City Bishop Zumárraga recounts in a letter to Emperor Charles V (June 12, 1531) that more than fifteen hundred temples and twenty thousand "idols" had been destroyed. On the other hand, anything unconnected with religion was lovingly preserved, like languages, daily usages and customs, and civil monuments. For more details see Ricard, *Conquista espiritual de México*, pp. 96–108; Specker, *Missionsmethode in Spanisch-Amerika*, pp. 116–35.

21. Cf. M. León-Portilla, *A conquista da América Latina vista pelos indios* (Petrópolis), p. 41.

22. Ibid., p. 48.

23. Ibid., p. 20.

24. Puebla says: "It is the Gospel, fleshed out in our peoples, that has brought them together to form the original cultural and historical entity known as Latin America. And this identity is glowingly reflected on the *mestizo* countenance of Mary of Guadalupe, who appeared at the start of the evangelization process" (Puebla Final Document, no. 446).

25. Cf. E. Hoornaert, "A evangelização segundo a tradição guadalupana," *Revista Eclesiástica Brasileira* 34 (1974): 524–45; C. Siller, *El método de la evangelización en el Nican Mopohua* (Mexico City, 1986).